How to build a

CLASSIC GOLF SWING

How to build a CLASSIC GOLF SWING

ERNIE ELS

with Steve Newell

Photography by

DAVE CANNON

Collins Willow

An Imprint of HarperCollins*Publishers*

First published in hardback in 1998 by CollinsWillow
an imprint of HarperCollins*Publishers*
London

First published in paperback in 1998

1 3 5 7 9 8 6 4 2

The Author asserts the moral right to be
identified as the author of this work

A CIP catalogue record for this book
is available from the British Library

ISBN 0 00 218900 3

Designed and produced by
Cooling Brown (*Book Packaging*)
9–11 High Street, Hampton, Middlesex TW12 2SA

Colour reproduction by
Colourscan, Singapore

Printed and bound in Italy by Eurografica

CONTENTS

FOREWORD

In over forty years playing professional golf, I've seen and played with an awful lot of good young golfers. A small number grew to become world-beaters. Some came on to the scene showing tremendous talent and promising great things, only to burn brightly for just a few years and then fade into the background. Others simply couldn't fulfil their potential. For whatever reason it might have been, they just didn't mature into really top players.

When I first saw Ernie Els play golf, though, I knew I was witnessing one of golf's next generation of superstars. Far from being just a one-minute wonder, I thought immediately here is a player who has everything. His size and build, combined with a truly classic golf swing, enables him to generate immense power that is both effortless and enviable. He has wonderful rhythm to his swing and, for someone so big, a lovely touch around the greens and a great putting stroke.

Since that first day I saw Ernie play, several years ago, nothing has happened to make me change my opinion of the big man. He has won several world titles and, in capturing the 1994 US Open at the relatively young age of 24, has claimed what I think will be his first of many major championships. Naturally, he is saddled with such titles as the 'next Jack Nicklaus' or the 'greatest South African since a certain Gary Player'. But 'the first Ernie Els' is a more apt and deserving tag. Of all the young golfers playing today, to my mind there is no one more capable of dominating the game of golf as it moves into the next millennium. He has every shot in the book and I believe there is nothing he cannot achieve if he puts his mind to it.

In addition to his qualities as a golfer, Ernie Els is a fine young man, an ideal role model for youngsters, and a person I like immensely. He has a mature head on those broad young shoulders and this has certainly played a major part in his success to date and will continue to aid him in the future. A strong mind is one of the key components that separates the great from the good.

It is for all these reasons that I am delighted to contribute to this, Ernie's first ever instruction book. Unusually for one so young, there is already much he can teach the average golfer. Just from studying the photographs alone, everyone playing the game can learn from Ernie's classic action. On top of this, he describes the golf swing in what I think is an in-depth, but easy-to-understand style. That sums up Ernie's game. He typifies the virtues of golf's basic fundamentals, but doesn't let them get in the way of him making a wonderfully free-flowing, rhythmical swing. In many ways, he plays a natural game

I sincerely hope you enjoy this book because I think a lot of Ernie's attitudes and thoughts on the golf swing shine through. I hope it gives you an edge over your playing partners and enables you to lower your personal best scores. And I also hope you'll enjoy watching Ernie Els play golf for many years to come. Because I know I most certainly will.

Gary Player

GARY PLAYER

South Africa, 1995

INTRODUCTION

I was incredibly lucky to be introduced to the game of golf at a young age – I remember being about eight years old when I first caddied for my dad at the local golf course. I started by bashing the odd ball around, but to be honest I was pretty useless until I was about 12 or 13. My dad never really pushed me into taking lessons – he just encouraged me to play my natural game for the first few years. So I basically had very few mechanical thoughts – I just 'let it happen'.

Even though I wasn't brilliant from day one, I liked what I saw straight away and it wasn't long before I was well and truly hooked. I loved everything about the game of golf and preferred it to all the other sports I'd tried. Looking back, I think one of the things that appealed to me most was that I saw golf as more of a personal challenge, and I still do. Just me against the course; I either win or I lose; I either shoot 65 or 75 – it's all down to me. On the bad days, I've got no one else to blame but myself. And on the good days, I can enjoy the glory – really enjoy it! – knowing that I did it all myself. That's the way I like it to be.

My enjoyment and keenness for golf was boosted, of course, by the fact that I started to improve rapidly in my early teens. As I said, I didn't actually have a coach, I just tried to learn things by watching players like Jack Nicklaus and Gary Player. I was small as a boy, so I couldn't always hit the ball a long way. However, I still managed to get down to scratch at the age of 14 and was enjoying the competitiveness and spirit of first team matches for my home club, Kempton Park, near Johannesburg. A year later I was world champion in my age group, winning the junior championship in California. Success came quickly and I was getting into the habit of winning, although I had no idea at the time how much that experience would help me in the years to come.

Even so, it wasn't all golf back then. I was also playing plenty of other sports: I was a useful rugby player (No.8, not surprisingly!) and I had also won the Senior Eastern Transvaal tennis championship in my early teens. My cricket wasn't too shabby, either. Bit by bit, though, golf started to put every other sport in the shade. I knew then that I wanted golf to be more than just a game for me.

When I eventually did turn pro in 1989 I honestly didn't know what to expect. A glittering amateur career doesn't always convert into pound signs when you turn pro. After a couple of fairly quiet years, things started to go well. I was taking my golf far more seriously, practising more and spending a little less time with my mates. I won the odd tournament here and there and that was a nice feeling. Then in 1992 I went crazy – I won the South African PGA, the South African Masters and the South African Open, the first person to win that trio of titles since Gary Player. That all happened in the space of a couple of months, and there were three other tournament wins thrown in for good measure, too. Of the 11 tournaments played on the 1992 South African Tour, I ended up winning six of them. What a year!

Then in the summer of 1992, I played in my first British Open (which was held at Muirfield, a really tough track) and opened up with a 66 followed by a 69. Not bad for a first attempt. Playing right up with the leaders at the weekend was another great learning experience and to be honest, come Sunday, I was pretty happy to finish fifth, just a handful of shots behind the eventual winner, Nick Faldo.

All in all, 1992 was a hell of a year. I was on a roll. I think it was then that I really felt I was capable of competing, and eventually beating, the best in the world. You have to prove those things to yourself, you have to really believe it, before it can actually happen.

A couple of years later I did prove it, making the big breakthrough by winning my first major, the US Open at Oakmont. To be honest, of the four majors the US Open was the one I least expected to win, simply because it places so much emphasis on straight hitting off the tee and I have a tendency to hit the occasional loose tee-shot. But it certainly was a nice surprise.

The reason I tell you all this is simple. Because for all the time I was making great strides in the game, I can honestly say that my golf swing changed very little. Sure, it may be a little more consistent and solid these days, but basically it has stayed the same. I've always felt that I had great rhythm in my swing and, combined with a pretty decent technique, when I was in the groove I stayed in the groove. There was no need to change anything – I just concentrated on my rhythm, made sure my set-up was always good and away I would go. And that's how it is today. Not too technical – I just swing it freely and smoothly.

And yes, I can hit the ball a long way, too. Now, when I play in pro-ams, that's one of the things I'm always being asked by club golfers. "How do you hit the ball so far with so little effort" they say. Well I can tell you now what I tell them on the course. There are no secrets – no magic formula. And forget buying distance. Sure, it's important that you have properly fitted clubs, but the latest fancy driver won't make a scrap of difference unless you know how to swing it. At the end of the day, it all comes down to the point of impact: getting the clubface to the ball, squarely, at the correct angle, on the correct path and, obviously, at speed.

That might sound like a lot of things to get right – particularly when everything is happening in little more than a split-second – but it's not as daunting as it sounds. The golf swing is like a chain reaction. Set up to the ball correctly and you're more likely to make a good takeaway. Make a good takeaway and your backswing will benefit. It really is a case of one good move leading to another. If you take the time to get the basics right, your chances of achieving good impact increase – and those fundamentals apply to every club in the bag.

What I want to do in this book is show you how you can fit together all the pieces that make up a good golf swing. I'm going to help you get the basics right more often – and believe me, that'll give you a better looking swing and a more effective one. I'm going to help your rhythm, too. And I'll also demonstrate how you can start to hit it further and straighter. Put this all together and you've got what I'd call a winning combination.

All the time you're playing the game, though, I want you to have fun as well. I'm sure it's one of the secrets to me playing well. Before a round I often say to my caddie, Ricky Roberts, "let's just go out there and enjoy it". If you can do that, even in a tournament, then you're half-way to playing better golf. This book will hopefully contribute the other half.

Keep swinging smoothly!

ERNIE ELS

South Afria, 1995

THE FUNDAMENTALS

The foundation of a classic golf swing

I can guess what you're thinking; all you want to do is hit balls and here I am starting off by talking about the fundamentals. The set-up isn't exactly the most exciting subject, is it? And you've heard it all before, right?

Well, even if you think you have heard all you need to know about the fundamentals, it really is impossible to ignore them. Even as much as I play and practise, I'm constantly looking at my grip, posture and aim. Golf is my living and I can't afford to take anything for granted. Like the old saying goes: "If the gun isn't aimed correctly, the bullet won't hit the target".

To begin, put down this book for a moment and get yourself a golf club. I strongly advise you to copy everything I'm about to show you – get used to the feeling of a secure, neutral grip and start to familiarise yourself with the sensation of a good posture. Working through these points with me, every step of the way, will help you to really appreciate the importance of getting the fundamentals right. Do this now and they'll soon become second nature.

The grip

We'll start with the grip. Now don't you go skipping past these pages – this is important. Over the following pages, we've printed photographs of my hands in life-size proportions, which I hope will help you appreciate the correct positioning on the club and also make it easier for you to copy them.

Before I explain to you how to grip the club properly, though, let me show you what happens if you grip the club badly. You may well see and read some things here that strike a chord in your own game.

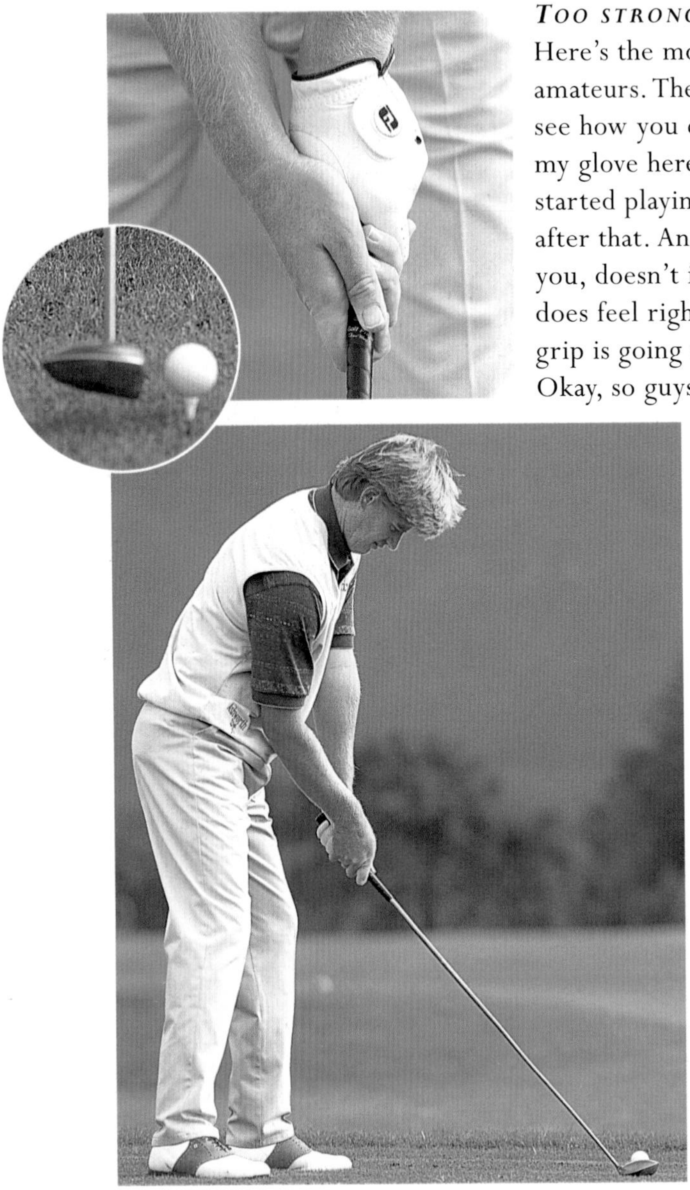

Too strong a grip

Here's the most common bad grip that I see in amateurs. The left hand is a little too strong – see how you can see more than two knuckles on my glove here. This is the grip I had when I started playing the game – and for a few years after that. And it probably feels comfortable for you, doesn't it? It did for me, too. But even if it does feel right, I can tell you now that a strong grip is going to hold you back, guaranteed. Okay, so guys like Fred Couples, Bernhard Langer and Paul Azinger make it work, but they are extremely talented. Personally, I'd much rather see you working on a neutral left-hand grip, just like the one I'm coming to in a page or two. It helped me improve back in my younger days and I know it will make it easier for you to build a classic, consistent golf swing.

To make matters worse, when you place your left hand on the grip too strong, the natural tendency is for your right hand to sit under the grip, also in a strong position. This

Gripping the club too strongly can lead to a closed clubface at impact (top) as well as a closed stance – look how it tucks my right shoulder in too low and behind me.

often leads to a closed stance – see how it tucks in my right shoulder, too low and behind me. If you were to draw a line along my shoulders it would point way right of target. That's going to encourage you to whip the club back on the inside – all shoulder-turn and no arm-swing. A bad start with more to follow.

As you will discover, if you try to swing with this grip, your hands have a natural tendency to return to square from a swinging motion – that's why we don't miss when we clap our hands together. The problem is that when your hands return to their more natural square position at impact, the clubface will almost certainly be totally shut. That means you'll struggle to hit the ball straight.

Too much in the palm

You should also make sure that the grip is not too much in the palm of your left hand. If you fall into that trap the results can be disastrous. It restricts the ability of your wrist to hinge correctly, which means you'll struggle to make a good move away from the ball. Just as damaging, this kind of grip will cost you speed through the ball which, in turn, will result in poor strikes, no accuracy and no distance.

A weak grip

You also need to make changes if you suffer from the slightly less common fault of having a weak grip. See, here, how my hands are too far to my left (or right as you're looking at me) on the grip. There are too many knuckles showing on my right hand – you can virtually see them all – and not enough showing on my left. This really is weak in every sense.

First, it leaves your shoulders open at address, which will certainly mean that you'll swing the club on an out-to-in path. That kind of language converts into big, ugly slices. The sort you hate. And the same principle applies to the position of your hands at impact. When you start from a weak position, the hands return to square at impact...which means the clubface is open. To stand any chance of getting the clubface square at impact, you are constantly having to correct yourself mid-swing. No matter how hard you try, you will never hit the ball solidly or consistently with this grip.

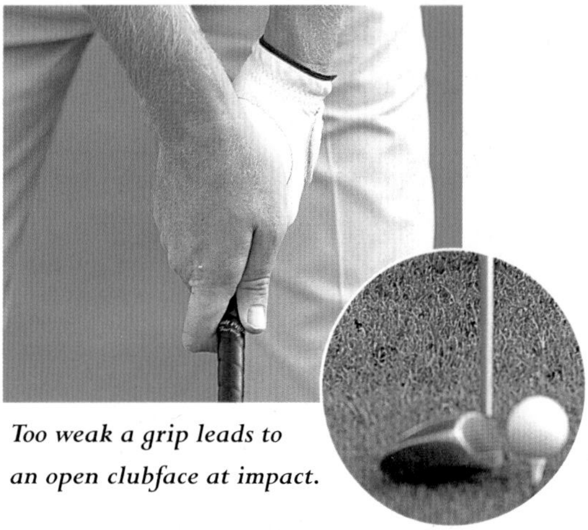

Too weak a grip leads to an open clubface at impact.

Getting a grip on your golf game

Now, over the following pages, let me show you how to grip it just like the pros do; a grip where both hands are encouraged to work together, in harmony, rather than fighting one another. Again, don't feel that you're too good a player to be reading this type of advice. Every golfer in the world – however long they might have been playing the game and however good they might think they are – can get nothing but good from checking their grip and fundamentals on a regular basis.

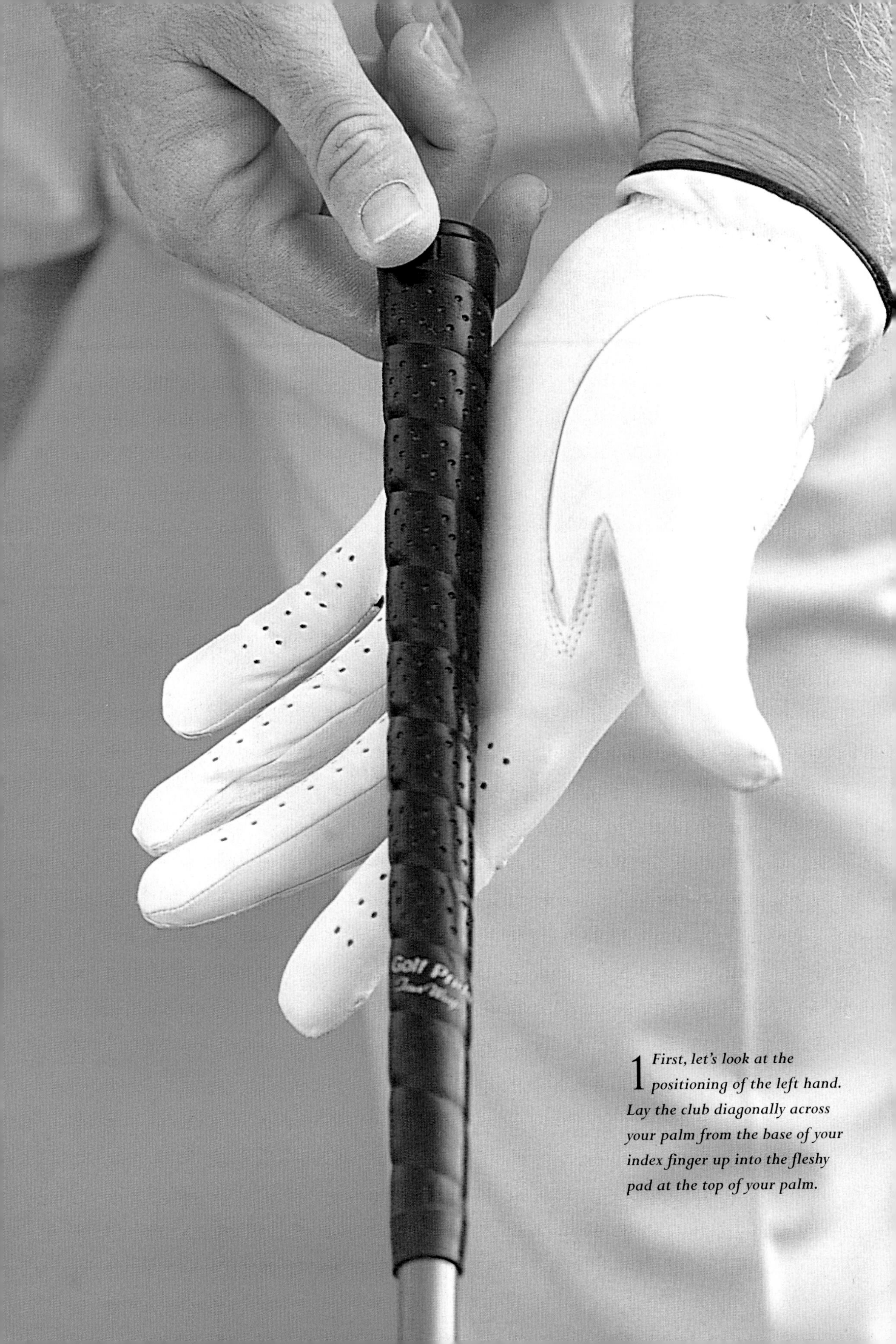

1 *First, let's look at the positioning of the left hand. Lay the club diagonally across your palm from the base of your index finger up into the fleshy pad at the top of your palm.*

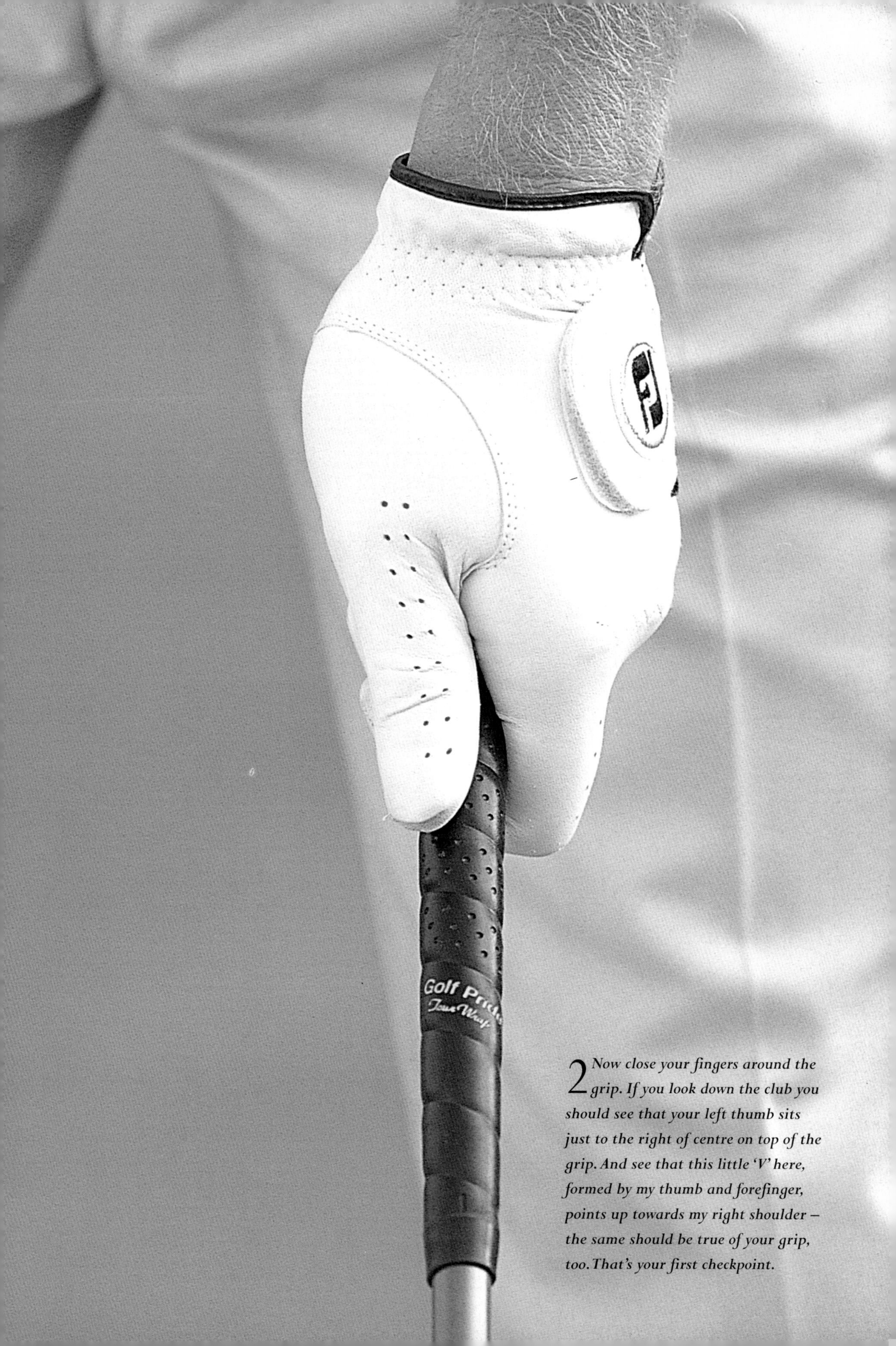

2 *Now close your fingers around the grip. If you look down the club you should see that your left thumb sits just to the right of centre on top of the grip. And see that this little 'V' here, formed by my thumb and forefinger, points up towards my right shoulder – the same should be true of your grip, too. That's your first checkpoint.*

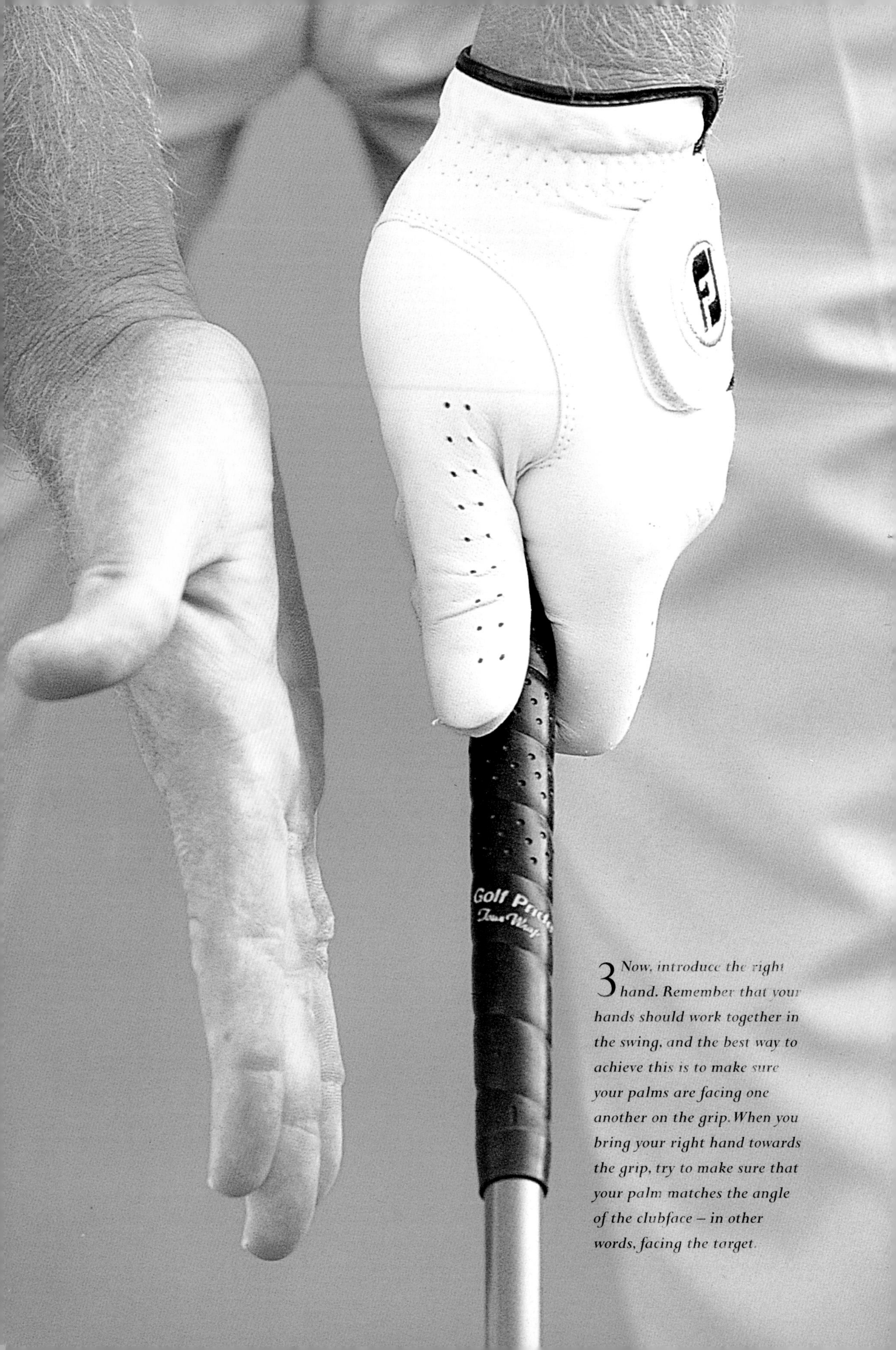

3 Now, introduce the right hand. Remember that your hands should work together in the swing, and the best way to achieve this is to make sure your palms are facing one another on the grip. When you bring your right hand towards the grip, try to make sure that your palm matches the angle of the clubface – in other words, facing the target.

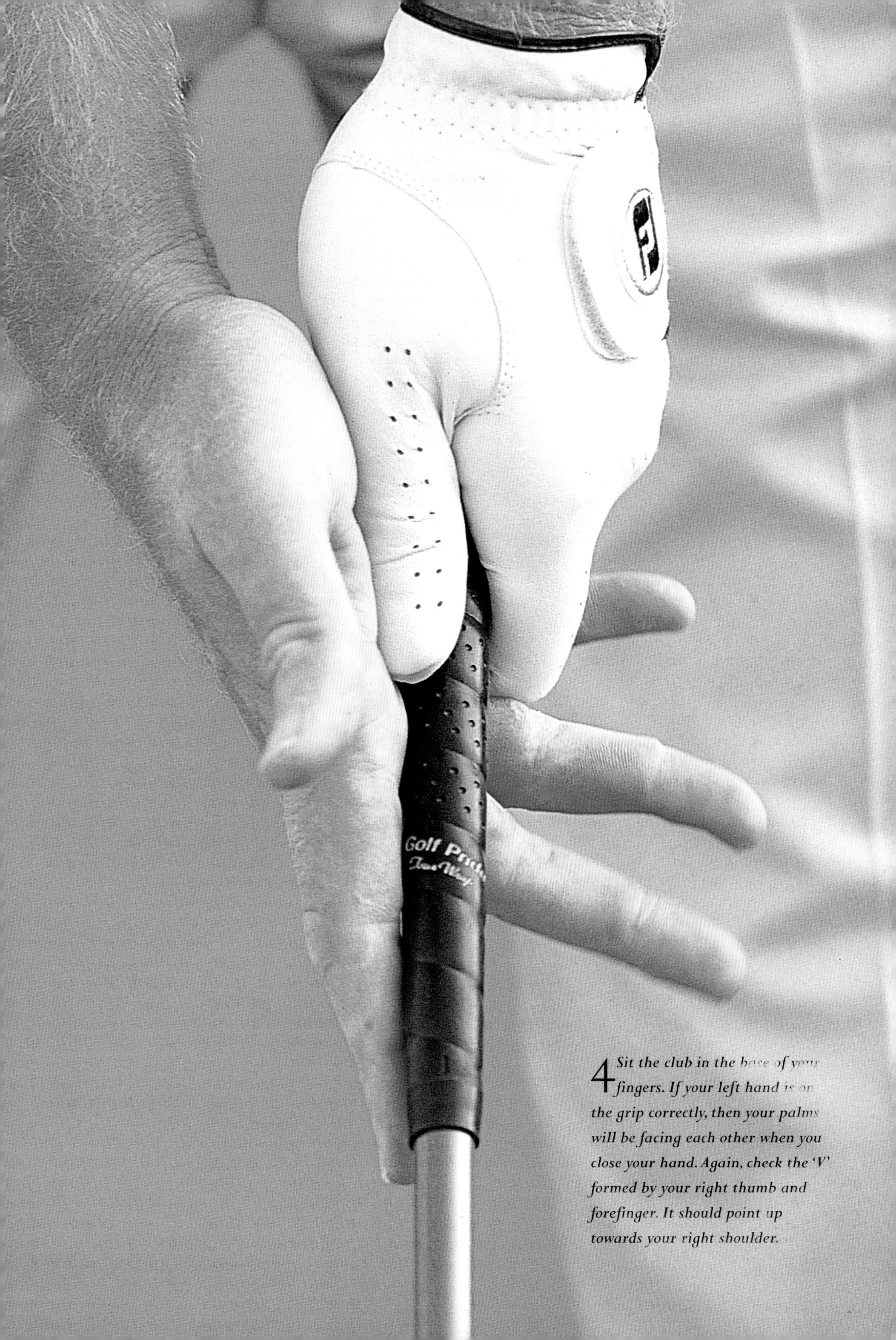

4 *Sit the club in the base of your fingers. If your left hand is on the grip correctly, then your palms will be facing each other when you close your hand. Again, check the 'V' formed by your right thumb and forefinger. It should point up towards your right shoulder.*

5 *Look at this 'trigger' position formed by my right index finger and thumb. You'll see this in every good player in the world. It gives your grip an added element of feel, security and power – so make sure you've got one. The grip really should feel quite secure in this trigger. Waggle the club back and forth with your hands – feel the sensation of your wrists hingeing and try to get a feel for the weight of the clubhead.*

Baseball grip

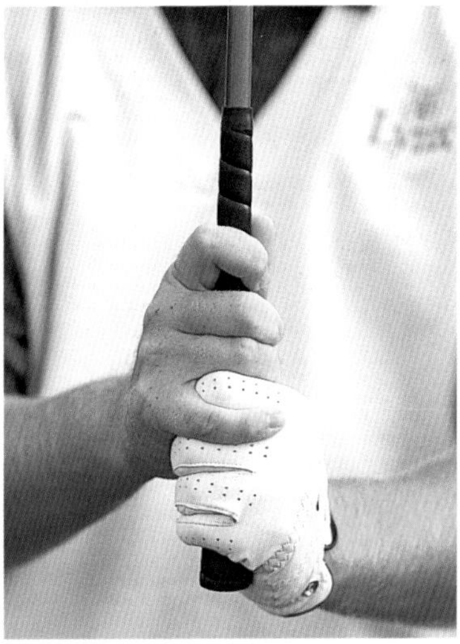

Overlapping grip

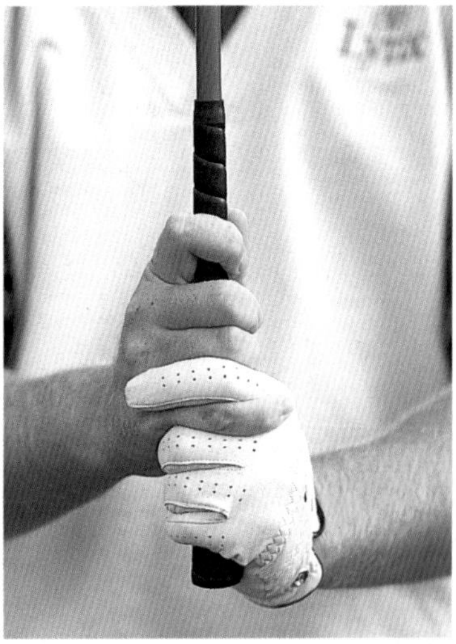

Interlocking grip

You probably don't need me to tell you there are three styles of grip – baseball (or two-handed), interlocking and overlapping. As a general guide, the baseball grip is good if you're a youngster and you don't have a great deal of strength in your wrists. It's also good if you have been playing sport all your life and are just starting to suffer the effects of arthritis or stiffness in your fingers. Overlapping is the most popular among professionals and is the one I have always used. The interlocking style is used mainly by players who have fairly small hands or short fingers – Jack Nicklaus and Tom Kite are two golfers who have used the interlocking grip to stunning effect. However, these guidelines aren't set in stone, so feel free to experiment.

One final thought on the grip. When you're working on these points I have covered, try to bear in mind that your grip is the hardest thing to change in golf. It's bound to feel strange at first (Ben Hogan said that if a grip change doesn't feel strange then you haven't made a change at all) and you'll hit some pretty strange shots as well. But if you persevere, I can't tell you how good it'll be for your game. With a good grip your hands will start to work together, as one unit; your wrists will hinge more easily and more effectively; and, perhaps most importantly of all, you'll find it easier to deliver the clubface square to the ball more frequently – and that means more accurate golf shots. So, while a grip change might not be a great deal of fun, the results most certainly are.

KEY TIP PLAY WITH YOUR BARE HANDS

Don't feel that you have to wear a glove for every shot you hit, certainly not just because everyone else at your club probably does. I know several decent amateur golfers who play with their bare hands and, of course, Freddie Couples and Corey Pavin (both major winners) don't do too badly without a gloved left hand. Even if you do prefer to wear a glove for the full shots, I certainly think it's a good thing to remove it for those delicate, short-range strokes – chips and putts, for instance. That's where you need all the feel you can get in your fingertips and a glove can sometimes hamper that feeling.

Aiming correctly

Remember what I said at the start of this chapter about aiming the gun and hitting the target. Well, that's as good a way as I can think of to describe the effect that aim and alignment both have on your swing and your golf shots. But while the theory makes absolutely perfect sense, you'll know yourself that when it comes to aim, it's easy to slip into bad habits.

How many times have you had a friend tell you on the tee that you're aiming 30yds (27m) right, when to you it feels like you're aiming dead-straight at the target? And then when you do try to straighten-up your alignment, it feels as though you're aiming 50yds (45m) left into the trees. Start letting your alignment slip here, and before you know it your aim is way out, particularly if you play only once or twice a week. What's more, all the time you're aiming incorrectly, you're having to make compensations in your swing to get the ball back on line. Effectively, you're actually practising your mistakes. So not only is your aim poor, but your swing is getting worse into the bargain. That kind of damage can take a long time to repair, so I reckon it's a lot easier to make sure you don't slip into those bad habits in the first place, and here's how you do it. Whenever you practise, always use a couple of clubs laying on the ground to ensure that your alignment and aim remain fairly constant. And I mean always. One club should run just outside, though parallel, to the ball-to-target line (you can then place the ball just inside of the shaft). Position the second club along the line of your toes, parallel to the other club. That's where the term parallel alignment comes from – the ideal position for hitting consistently solid, straight shots. Your shoulders and hips should also run along a line parallel to the target.

Your toes, hips and shoulders all run along a line parallel to the target.

As an extra check, try this quick drill. Set-up to the ball and hold the shaft of the club along your thighs. Now look down that shaft and you will be able to see what line your lower body is on. Whether it's dead straight, right or left, you'll spot it easily and immediately, and therefore know exactly what adjustments are required. Obviously you can't go performing those kind of tricks out on the course – you'd pick up a heap of penalty shots, for one thing. But if you do these exercises often enough, you should find that aiming correctly becomes more of a routine job when you're on the course.

That's why professional golfers get it right more often than not. It's a case of repetition breeding good habits and means that you're much less likely to make a mistake when it matters most. And that's bound to help you hit more straight shots.

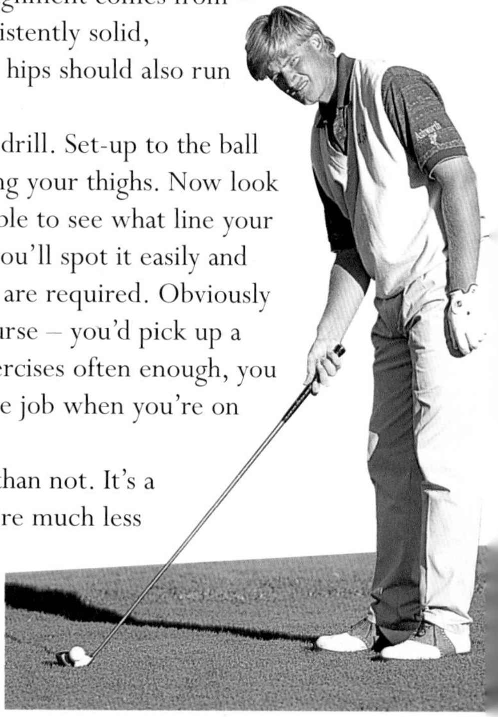

Check the alignment of your knees and feet by holding the shaft of a club across your thighs.

As you can see, it will quickly become apparent when you're aiming too far right...

...or if your aim has strayed too far to the left from perfect parallel alignment.

KEY TIP CLUBFACE AIM IS VITAL

As you take your address position, try to get into the habit of first aiming the clubface at the target and then building your stance around that. Watch someone like Greg Norman perform this exact routine – how meticulously he aims the clubface and how he then steps in to his final address position. It's a very precise, consistent pre-shot routine and the clubface is the key to Greg finding the correct address position.

There are plenty of other methods, of course, for setting up to the ball. For the average player, though, I think the 'clubface first, feet second' routine is the easiest to repeat on a consistent basis. I also think that correct clubface aim is one of the most important aspects of the golf swing. So it's crucial that you start by getting that right – then you can worry about everything else. You might also try aiming the clubface over an intermediate target between the ball and the flag, just as many professionals on tour do.

Of course, you don't have to follow Greg's lead, but it is vital to have some form of method, and one that feels comfortable and easy to repeat. Never casually plant your feet in and settle down before aiming the clubface. Do this and you'll never achieve consistent aim or alignment.

Correct clubface aim is vital to accurate golf shots. So make sure you first place the club behind the ball, with perfect aim (far left). Then move into your final address position. This routine helps ensure perfect parallel alignment.

Developing a great posture

Another crucial element of a good set-up is your posture. If you look at me, at 6ft 3in tall and nearly 16 stone, I'm not the ideal build for golf (I'm more like a rugby player, if anything). However, my posture has always been good. Basically, I learnt the value of good posture early on and have played by those rules ever since. Because I never let it slip, I never had any of the problems that tall players can sometimes experience.

When I play in pro-ams, which I do nearly every week of the year, I see very few amateurs with really good posture. To be honest, I think it's something that the average club golfer just isn't aware of. Unfortunately, that's a big mistake. Your posture influences the shape and quality of your entire swing. If your posture is poor, my guess is that your swing will be poor too. On the other hand, if I see a golfer with good posture at address then, more often than not, they'll make a pretty good swing from there. That's how important it really is.

So what makes good posture?

Let's look at the angle of the spine first as this is what determines the plane of your swing. That's why a small guy like Ian Woosnam will always have a flatter swing plane than someone like me or, to take an extreme example, Andy North. Woosie stands fairly upright to the ball and so swings more around his body. Tall guys have to bend over more at the waist, so the club is bound to travel on more of a straight-up-and-down plane.

So whenever you get your mind in a twist about what might be the ideal swing plane for you, my advice is to review your spine angle and overall posture, and check that it's spot-on. Your swing plane will take care of itself. Certainly, don't tie yourself in knots about this subject, as it can do you more harm than good.

How to assess your own posture

If you're not sure what the ideal spine angle is for you, try rehearsing this simple exercise. And don't do it just once in a blue moon. Repeat it over and over again, between hitting shots, until it starts to feel really comfortable. That's the key.

So, stand up straight with your arms hanging down by your side and your heels spread roughly shoulder-width apart. For now I suggest you use the driver, as I am here.

Now hold the club out in front of you at roughly shoulder-height. Start to bend from the waist, ever-so slowly, and at the same time feel that you stick out your backside a little. Sense that you're easing yourself on to a very high stool and *sit down a little*. As you do this, make a real effort to keep your back nice and straight. Keep bending until the clubhead makes contact with the ground. You should feel now that your hands and arms simply hang down in front of you, quite

naturally and very relaxed, without a hint of any tension. Finally, flex your knees, introducing a little bit of tension into your thighs. That is bound to feel strange at first, but once you've repeated this exercise a few times it will start to feel more natural. You've now established good posture and the correct spine angle.

JUST RELAX

A final word about that well worn phrase I'm sure you've heard a thousand times – *just relax*. I can understand people's good intentions when they say this, but the trouble with this little 'gem' of advice is that many golfers try too hard to relax. Some guys I see look like the wind might blow them over – they're all hunched and sloppy, and that's not what is meant by *just relax*.

The best way I can tell you to relax is to start from your hands up. You already know how to grip the club. Just make sure you don't grip too tightly – sense that your hands fit snugly and securely around the grip, like you were holding a child's hand. This ensures that your arms aren't too tense, which in turn ensures that your shoulders aren't tense, either. That's the kind of relaxed feeling which is good for your golf – it spreads throughout your entire body. And all this is built around a good posture.

Finally, keep your head up away from your chest. I cringe when I hear someone say 'keep your head down' – it's got to be one of the worst pieces of advice in golf. If you keep your head down, it stops your shoulders from turning and encourages a reverse pivot in the backswing, signalling disaster. So, at address always think 'chin up' and feel like you're looking down your nose at the ball. You will find that it gives you much more room to turn your left shoulder in behind the ball.

KEY TIP LOOK DOWN THE LINE

When you've settled into your position, hang a club straight down from the centre of your right shoulder and look down the line of the shaft, just like I'm doing here. If it hangs down through a point level with your knee-cap, then you're in good shape. However, if it's either side of that, then you're doing something wrong and it's time to make a subtle adjustment.

Weight distribution and ball position

The only things left to cover now as far as your set-up is concerned are weight distribution and ball position. For now, I'll again deal specifically with the driver. I'll talk about all of your other clubs later in the book.

Most of you will have been told to spread your weight evenly on the balls of both feet. Well, I agree with the part about feeling your weight is over the balls of your feet. And spreading it evenly on both feet is also fine with most clubs. But not with the driver. Personally, I prefer to have my weight favouring the right side just a touch – roughly a 60:40 ratio – to encourage a better turn away from the ball and a good transfer of weight on to the right side in the backswing. I suggest you do the same; it'll be good for your turn and help prevent you reverse pivoting in the backswing, which, as I've said, is one of the biggest 'distance killers' in golf.

I mentioned earlier the ideal system for determining the right width of stance for you. It's simple, but like many of the fundamentals of golf, so often ignored. Just stand in front of a full-length mirror, or a window, and check that the insides of your heels (not the outsides of your feet) are shoulder-width apart.

This forms the perfect base to swing around. Any narrower than that and you're going to sway from side to side like a young tree in the wind and you'll never hit the ball solidly. Any further apart than shoulder-width and you have zero chance of making a good turn in the backswing. Even if you're extremely supple, believe me you'll struggle. Again, though, the shoulder-width rule applies only with the driver and long irons. For shorter shots played with the pitching-wedge and sand-wedge, which I will deal with in greater detail later in the book, your stance will need to become a little narrower.

Positioning the ball

Strange as it may seem to some of you, ball position is one of the key thoughts of my set-up. The positioning of the ball and my alignment are the two areas that my whole swing revolves around, and it needs to be for you as well. It's absolutely vital to my game and I can't exaggerate how important it is.

Using the driver, the ball should be in one place, and one place only, opposite the inside of your left heel. That gives you the best possible chance to sweep the ball away, clean as a whistle, off the tee-peg, which is the ideal contact to aim for with the driver. Any further back towards the middle of your stance and you're in trouble – you'll almost certainly have a tendency to hit down on the ball too steeply. That may be okay with a 9-iron, but a driver…man, you're going to have serious problems. Placing the

With the ball too far forward in your stance, you'll never hit solid drives.

The ball too far back in your stance causes an excessively steep angle of attack.

ball too far back in your stance also 'shuts down' your stance, causing you to aim too far right all the time.

If, on the other hand, you position the ball too far forward, say, just ahead of your left toe, then you're going to have the complete opposite problems. For a start, you'll have a tendency to align your upper body left of target – that's a natural reaction. You'll also be reaching for the ball at impact – the ball is so far forward you'll be hitting it too much on the upswing. The chances are that you'll either top it or, even if you do manage to hit the ball cleanly, achieve no real penetration in the ball-flight. So keep that ball position up around your left heel – as I say, I can't stress how vital it is.

Now reading this section you may think that this is a lot to worry about. I know it can seem that way, but that's really not the case. In fact, the opposite is true. You do need to pay attention to these fundamentals on the practice ground, but this is so that you don't have to worry about them on the course.

All the time you are working towards getting to the stage where a good set-up and posture become almost second nature. That leaves your mind free to worry about choosing the right club and hitting the right shots at the right time. In other words, the name of the game. You're never too good a player to work on the fundamentals. Just ask any golfer on any tour in the world today.

KEY TIP

STARTING OFF ON THE RIGHT FOOT

When you're at the golf range, or on the practice ground, always make a point of checking your ball position before you hit your first shot. Whatever club you ordinarily use to start off your practice session (I wouldn't use anything longer than a 7- or 8-iron) make sure you get that ball position absolutely spot-on. Remember, one good thing leads to another in golf – and the chain reaction starts with your address position. This will help ensure that you don't start your practice sessions by practising a mistake.

The pre-shot routine – breeding good habits

In terms of its influence on the golf swing, the pre-shot routine is underestimated – hugely so in my opinion. A consistent pre-shot routine is something that you see every professional do. You may not be aware of it, but look out for it next time there's a tournament on the television. Pick out a player, and then watch how they approach every shot. It never varies and usually follows roughly this pattern: they stand behind the ball, visualise the shot, address the ball, have the same number of waggles every time, and then pull the trigger. It's almost like clockwork.

In contrast to this, I see few amateurs who actually have a routine, let alone a consistent one. Often their pre-shot routine will depend on how the round is going. On a bad day, with the scorecard in tatters, there will be no routine at all. And on a good day, they'll spend an age choosing clubs and lining up putts. Neither one is ideal because neither is consistent. If you don't have a pre-shot routine, you're missing out on a great opportunity.

The first thing I want you to do, then, is develop a routine, based on the one I've just described in this chapter, and which I'm following in the photographs on the opposite page. Don't worry, it doesn't have to be an identical routine, but it's a useful guide and it works for a lot of the top players. Now make sure you repeat it every time you prepare to hit a shot. Before long, you won't have to think too hard about it – the routine will become just that – routine. Almost second nature, in fact.

This is going to help your golf game a lot, believe me. It's one of the best ways I know to help you cope with pressure because it focuses your mind as you shape up to hit a shot. When the 'heat is on' you can go through your normal routine and learn to treat it just like any other shot.

Focus your mind on the shot you're about to play and pick out an ideal landing spot.

Settle the club down and aim the clubface at your intended target.

Once the clubface is aimed correctly, build your stance around it.

With everything in place, you are then ready to pull the trigger...

...and watch as the ball launches away down the fairway.

The Classic Swing – Driver

How to hit long and straight tee shots

Now you're all set, with the seeds of golf's fundamentals firmly planted in your mind, let's get down to the serious business of hitting some balls. As we work through this section, I want you to think about what I said in my introduction to the book – that the golf swing is a chain reaction. If you make one good move, then it generally leads to another and that's why the fundamentals I've just described to you are so important. Make sure you are certain you have a good grasp of *G.A.S.P.* – grip, aim, stance and posture. They're each going to make your life a good deal easier on the course.

Here, I'm going to break down the swing into key stages, one-by-one. Then you can appreciate fully the whole chain reaction process. Again, I suggest you grab a club and copy what I'm doing, trying to emulate each position, though it's a good idea to pause as you reach each stage. Even better, rehearse these moves in front of a mirror so that you can compare what you feel with what you actually see. That's an important step towards understanding your own golf swing.

In a way, you're training your body to behave in the way it should, rather than the way you have grown used to. You can feel a good takeaway, see a good top of the backswing position, understand how to start the downswing and swing through the hitting zone correctly. Fitting together all the elements of a good swing is rather like putting together a jigsaw – and it can make for a pretty picture when you're finished.

Remember, when you're out on the course, never consciously try to swing to each of these positions. That'll inhibit the flowing movement of your swing and stop you striking the ball properly. Just concentrate on setting up to the ball correctly, again with good posture, then think rhythm and tempo. Trust your 'muscle memory' to take over.

Posture alert!

Right, I don't want you to move a muscle until I'm certain your posture and set-up are in great shape. So let's make a quick pre-flight check. You may be thinking 'oh, not again'. but seriously, it really can make a big difference. First, concentrate on going through your normal pre-shot routine – and don't worry, it won't be long before you'll be performing this on auto-pilot.

Now settle in over the ball. Rehearse again the posture exercise I demonstrated to you on pages 24 and 25. Once in position, make sure your back is pretty straight; your spine angled forwards from the hips to encourage your arms to hang down in a relaxed, comfortable fashion. Feel that flex in your knees, the tension in your thighs, and your weight favouring your right side just a fraction. And remember to grip the club nice and lightly. If you've worked at this often enough since reading it for the first time, it should now be starting to feel pretty comfortable. That's a very positive sign because it's going to improve the shape and quality of your golf swing.

Ashworth

The first link in the chain

How you start the swing will determine just how well it continues. So your first move away from the ball – or to put it another way, the first link in the chain – is obviously very important. It sets a pattern, either good or bad, that the rest of your swing tends to follow.

For me, the first part of the takeaway is all arms. With every club in the bag – from the driver right down to the sand-wedge – I feel that my arms sweep the clubhead away from the ball 'wide and slow'. My wrists don't hinge – that comes later. At this stage it's all arms. This motion starts to pull my left shoulder, my left hip and left knee in towards the ball, causing my upper body to show the first signs of that all-important turning action. A perfect start.

Again, work with me on this one. Address the ball and sweep the clubhead away from it 'wide and slow'. Get used to this sensation of the arms leading the way and your left side being pulled in towards the ball. This is what's referred to in golfing circles as the one-piece takeaway. Everything moves away together; there's no independent hand action or excessive body motion, and the club, hands and arms are moving as one.

This gives you the width that you need in the swing; for the wider the arc is, the further the club travels in the swing. And the further the club travels, then the more power is generated in the swing, increasing the distances that the ball flies.

From the picture on the opposite page, looking straight down my target line, you can see one of the reasons why good alignment is so important. It helps me start the clubhead back on the correct path; straight back for the first 18in (45cm) or so, before arcing inside in harmony with the turning motion of my body.

PATH AND PLANE

Make sure that your own swing follows the same track and, as you do, make a conscious effort to keep the clubhead outside your hands going back. This again helps prevent any loose connections in the takeaway, such as your wrists 'collapsing', while the shaft stays on the correct plane going back, too.

A subtle rotation of your left forearm – which will happen virtually automatically if your grip is correct – will keep the clubface square to the path of your swing going back. That's obviously a good thing because you don't have to make any compensatory moves later in the swing to get it back to square. So far so good, then.

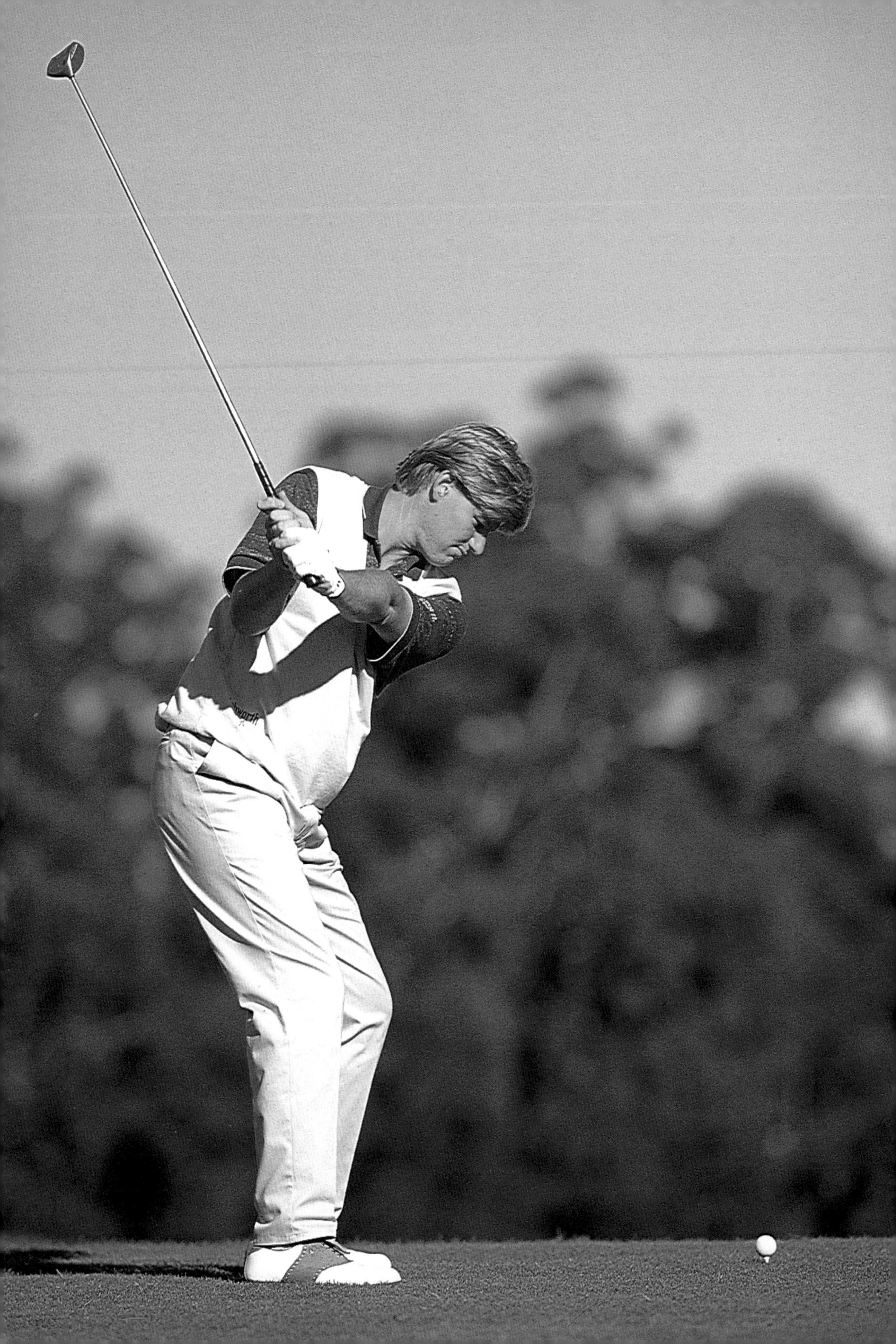

Combine a swing and hinge

As your arms continue to swing, and your body continues to rotate, let your wrists hinge freely so that the club points up towards the sky, and slightly behind you. Check this move in a mirror: by the time your left arm reaches a position horizontal to the ground, the shaft of the club should form a 90° angle. For some golfers, such as Jack Nicklaus and Greg Norman, this 90° angle appears a fraction later in the backswing – mainly because they take the club away so wide. I'm not saying that's a bad thing – in fact it has it's advantages – but I do think for the average player it is best to look for this angle when your left arm reaches horizontal with the ground. A fraction later, if you must, but certainly never any earlier because that will make your swing too narrow. Remember, I'm talking about full shots here; things are slightly different with a shorter swing.

Looking at the same stage in the swing from down the target line, the shaft is said to be on plane when a line extended through the butt-end of the shaft strikes the ground approximately mid-way between your feet and the ball. This is known as being 'in the slot', and now you can play.

Just to remind you again, all this is made possible by having a good grip and a good set-up. Checking this position in a mirror is fine, but I also suggest that you get a friend to look at some of these positions in your swing while out on the course. As I have already mentioned, sometimes in golf, what you feel you are doing is a world apart from what you are actually doing. By getting someone to stand just where the camera is here, you can tell him what you're looking to achieve and have him confirm whether you're getting it right or not. That's a very worthwhile exercise.

Also, by this stage of the swing you should really feel your weight flowing over on to your right side. While this is happening, the body continues to rotate and the hips start to follow the lead. If I were to suggest one other thing to focus on at this point, it would be to make very sure that your right knee retains its original flex. You should almost feel the tension building up in your thigh. You don't want that leg to straighten in the slightest – if that happens your backswing loses all the control and power that it is supposed to be storing up in readiness for attacking the ball in the downswing.

Crank it all the way to the top

Now you simply need to turn your body to complete the backswing. If the first part of the takeaway is 'all arms' then the completion of the backswing is 'all shoulders'.

This final move in the backswing then slots the club into the perfect position at the top, with the shaft parallel to the target line, and your right wrist and left thumb under the shaft. Another point to look for in your own swing is that the back of your left hand matches the angle of the clubface. One of the benefits of a good, neutral grip. These are all finer details – certainly you can't, and shouldn't, think of things like this as you hit shots – but they are all worth checking whenever you can remember. It's just like giving your swing a regular service – you are helping to keep it running smoothly.

Looking at me face-on, you can see the presence of a good, powerful upper-body coil. That's where I get my power from. Check in your own swing that your upper body is fully coiled – the shoulders turned 90° and the hips 45°. What I would say is that the ratio of 90:45 is a textbook figure. As you can see, I turn my shoulders through more than 90°, and my hips slightly less than 45°. That's because I'm young and a lot more supple than the average person. If you can achieve this 'power' ratio you will generate greater torque and clubhead speed and hit the ball a long, long way. But don't pull a muscle trying it.

And don't feel that you have to keep your left heel planted to the ground in the backswing. If it helps you make a more complete turn, then lifting your left heel is a good idea. It should happen in response to the turning motion of your upper body, though, so don't make a conscious effort to lift it too soon.

CREATE RESISTANCE

Once again, remember to keep that right knee flexed. This holds your backswing in check, stops the right side spinning out of control, and helps create the feeling of resistance as you stretch your upper body in the backswing – rather like winding up a spring. If you let that right leg straighten in the backswing, it's like snapping the tension in a spring. Your body is turning into nothing and there's no resistance to support your upper body motion. And where there's no support, there's no power.

I want you to rehearse the last two stages of the swing as much as possible. Get yourself into the half-way back position, with your wrists hinged and the club at a 90° angle with your left arm, and get used to the feeling of turning your body to finish the backswing. Go on, keep doing it. With practice you'll get into perfect position every time.

The magic move – golf's power generator

The subtle transition from completing the backswing to starting the downswing is a major problem for the majority of golfers, and I have a good idea why. At this stage of the swing many golfers begin to have a nagging thought: "What moves first? The hands, the arms, the legs, hips, shoulders, the club? Everything?"

There are certainly plenty of options, and that, I believe, is the root of the problem. There seem to be so many different things to think about that your mind can easily become muddled, the result being that you rush what is probably the most important half-second in golf – and then you're in big trouble.

So let's sort out this problem together, once and for all. The late Harvey Penick, a great teacher and guru to some of today's best players, used to refer to this part of the swing as golf's 'Magic Move'. Well, he might call it magic, but believe me, anyone can perform this trick.

To help you get this right – because you need to if you want to hit great golf shots – I'm going to bring you back to the chain reaction theory again. Assuming you've got to the top of the backswing in good shape, with the majority of your body-weight supported over your right side, I want you to think of starting the downswing by simply dropping your arms and the club down onto the same path that you swung it back on. Just slot it into position and retain that angle between your left wrist and the shaft of the club. To condense this into one, neat phrase, just think "right elbow down to right side". You can see that happen in my swing, on the opposite page. Copy this and it will help ensure that you drop the club down on the correct plane.

As you do this, sense that there's a subtle shifting of your weight towards your left side. It's a gradual process, so don't rush it, and don't jump at the ball. Feel as though you almost 'squat down' – rather like you're re-centring your weight in readiness for a sudden jolt. This is another move that should be repeated over and over again. Swing it the top and make your magic move, just as I've described it. Right elbow to your right side and settle your weight. Don't go any further into your downswing until you're happy with what you're doing here.

Retain the power angle

Forget the different swing shapes that you see on tour, the different builds, heights and ages – for now, they mean nothing. Because if you were to look at every good player in the world at about this stage in the swing – and indeed, all the way through to impact – they would all look pretty much the same. Really try to store this image in your mind. There is no bail-out here; to hit great shots you've got to get this position right.

Making a good 'magic move' is going to really help at this stage, because a good deal of what you see in the 'hitting zone' is a reaction to what happens from the top of your backswing, rather than simply being an independent action. Still, we're breaking the swing down into pieces here, so let's talk about the key feelings and sensations that you should strive to achieve.

First of all, make sure that you retain the 'power angle' between your left forearm and the shaft of the club – this is where you store up all the clubhead speed. If you lose this angle too soon, then you will lose your speed through the ball and that is bound to cost you distance.

Sense that, as your downswing continues, you pull your left shoulder away from your chin. That's a tough thing to grasp, so just repeat it a few times with me. The moment you start the downswing you should sense the gap between your left shoulder and your chin widening. This process continues all the way through to impact.

I hope you can understand that, by using my body correctly in the swing, this enables me to drop the club into the ideal position from which to deliver the clubhead squarely to the ball, at maximum speed and at the perfect angle of attack.

Try it again: your left shoulder should be under your chin at the top of the backswing and from there you simply widen the gap. This instinctively helps you unwind your upper body, like the uncoiling of a powerful spring.

Once you start to successfully combine the rotary action with a good arm swing, one where you retain the power angle, then you're really going to notice a difference not just in the amount of power you can generate, but also the quality and consistency of ball-strike.

Your body opens up at impact

This is where it all happens, impact – the moment of truth for every shot. Everything you do in your golf swing for the rest of your life should be channelled into achieving the perfect impact rather like I have done here. So let me go through the key ingredients of a good, powerful impact position and tell you about a couple of the things you should feel at this crucial point in the swing.

First, and most importantly, note how the clubface is square to my intended target line and my hips and shoulders are open to the target line. That's just as it should be, so ignore anyone who says you have to be square at impact – the only thing that should be square at impact is the clubface. If you were to swing into a position where your body was square at impact, you couldn't release the clubhead through the ball with any power or direction.

Let me emphasize this again, your body has to be open to the target at the point of impact. To give you a good example of this, try throwing a ball and note what you do. You plant your feet a comfortable distance apart, draw your arm back and sway to the right. Then, as you bring your hand and arm forwards to release the ball, your body position is open.

This happens naturally because it is the only way you can generate any power. The same is true in the golf swing. The body has to be open to give your hands and arms sufficient room to swing down that line, freely and powerfully. That energy is then transferred into the club and into the ball. If your body is square, the arms will have nowhere to go.

Returning to my position, note how my weight is predominantly on my front foot. I'm afraid many amateurs seem to hang back on their right side in an attempt to lift the ball skywards, invariably resulting in topped and sliced shots all over the golf course. Instead, let your weight follow the swinging motion of the clubhead. In other words, in the downswing make sure your body-weight flows gradually from your right side over on to your left foot.

Hopefully, one of the things you'll learn in this section is that, with a good swing, you can simply trust the loft on the club to create the required amount of height for you. If your ball position is correct, the clubhead will sweep the ball off its tee-peg, clean as a whistle.

Finally, cast your mind back to the section that covered the grip. A good grip is what makes a good impact possible. It enables to you to swing the club freely and deliver the clubface absolutely bang-square to the ball at impact. So if ever you think that working on your grip is a little boring, think ahead to this impact position, because this is what a good grip can do for your golf game.

Release the club through the ball

This position here is basically an extension of good impact. And I mean 'extension' in every sense. There is good extension of my arms through the ball – in a free-flowing swing, centrifugal force takes care of that. There is also good extension in the sense that I'm in this position as a result of getting everything right before impact. So let's take a look at what this stage is all about.

Most importantly, note how my right hand crosses over my left through impact, indicating a powerful, free release of the clubhead. A nice swing thought that will help you release the clubhead properly is to imagine your left forearm rotating anti-clockwise through impact.

Looking down my target line on the opposite page, you can just about see that the shaft of the club, when it reaches horizontal, is also parallel with my target-line. This again is further proof of a good release combined with an effective body action. The club is moving so fast here that my arms effectively overtake my body through impact, although the body still continues to rotate as the arms swing up and around.

As I say, there's really not a lot else you can do in this area of the swing – it's more of a reaction than an action. Your head should naturally start to come up in order to follow the flight of the ball. But you shouldn't really have to think about this, just as you shouldn't attempt to keep your head down for too long. You will find that it comes up instinctively as you drive your right shoulder past your chin while your arms pull your body up and around into the followthrough position.

Unfortunately, I have to tell you the grim news that if you're in a bad position this late in the swing – with the club travelling so fast and the ball long gone – then it is too late to do anything about the ball you are probably about to lose! Because everything is happening so fast in the downswing, your mind doesn't have nearly enough to time to make decisions about changing position, or manipulating your hands or the clubhead.

If there's something wrong through impact, you will have to take a close look at what happens before impact to seek a remedy.

Free-wheel to a finish

I know a lot of golfers who think the followthrough position in the swing is totally unimportant. After all, the ball is long gone. Well, they are right about the ball being long gone, but they are most certainly wrong about everything else. The followthrough is extremely important. And I'll tell you why.

I think the followthrough position can reveal a lot about a person's golf swing. It's almost like a signature – every line, every flourish, revealing something about the character of the swing. With most good golfers, there are several things you can pin-point that tell you they are a good player. Take my followthrough position as an example.

Although static images aren't the best device for illustrating this point, my balance is spot-on. Even when I go for the big one off the tee, I never feel I'm stumbling off balance in the finish or rocking from side to side. My swing is under control, and if I were asked to do so, I could hold this pose for as long as I like.

That's something every amateur would do well to copy. Always swing within yourself, hold your finish...and watch it fly. Try to keep your balance and imagine that you're posing for a photograph. Just as I can, so you should be able to hold your followthrough position for as long as you like. If you can't, then there has to be something wrong.

Note how my weight is supported almost entirely on my left foot. From being pretty much on my right side at the top of the backswing, it has flowed gradually towards the target, in time with the swinging motion of my arms and the club. That's the way your weight should flow, too.

You can see that my right shoulder is the closest part of my body to the target, something I believe is very important in any swing. Firing your right shoulder through towards the target helps get you 'through' the ball – you don't get stuck on your right side in the downswing. From my point of view, it also helps prevent me from leaning back in the 'reverse-C' position...something I still have to guard against, being a tall person.

Ashworth

Summing up

That's the followthrough, then. Not so unimportant after all, is it? And that's the swing in its entirety. Hopefully, over the last 22 pages you will have learnt a bit about my swing and a great deal more about your own swing. By showing you how and why things happen, rather than merely explaining to you what the ideal positions are, I hope you now have a good understanding of the full 'chain reaction' theory – and also what ingredients make up an effective, consistent golf swing.

I also hope that you have the time to work through the swing with me, time and time again, and rehearse each of the stages I've demonstrated here. Try to make them a matter of habit. Try to get comfortable with every position. Then try to string them together, slowly at first, building up to full speed without a ball. Then put a ball down on the ground and give it a rip. I think you'll enjoy what you see.

Key tips for a classic swing

Why you should waggle

Once you're over the ball, I think it's really important that you have a swing trigger; something that helps you make a smooth first move and prevents you freezing over the ball. Every good player has one: Jack Nicklaus waggles the club slowly and then turns his head to the right just before he starts the swing; Gary Player kicks in his right knee; Arnold Palmer makes a couple of fast waggles. Jose Maria Olazabal doesn't waggle at all but there's just the hint of a forward-press before he 'fires the gun'. Me, I'm just happy making a couple of slow, smooth waggles of the clubhead.

I reckon it's vital for you to develop a trigger, and, whatever method you ultimately go with, I suggest you combine it with a good waggle of the club. It doesn't much matter how many, or how few, times you do it – just make sure you do. It helps stop you gripping the club tightly and getting too tense in your arms and shoulders. It can also be a useful mini-preview to the swing itself; you can get used to the feeling of the clubhead moving away, and approaching the ball, on the correct path and angle of attack. So, get yourself a waggle and stick to it with every shot you play. It is yet another area that will soon become second nature and another that's going to help your game, guaranteed.

Try to imagine the toe of the club passing the heel.

Make the toe pass the heel

Out on the golf course, factors such as wind speed, pin position, distance to the flag and any hazards can play havoc with your decision making. Unfortunately, doubt or second-guessing over the ball, can lead to you getting too tentative and too defensive. That usually results in a weakly struck shot where all you are doing is trying to guide the ball towards the target. That's not good enough. If you try to guide the ball, the exact opposite will happen – you'll lose accuracy.

So, to help guarantee a good, positive release of the club when you're out on the course, try to imagine the toe of the club passing the heel through impact. That simple mental imagery should ensure that you release the club properly through the ball and that will lead to a more penetrating flight and all-round better golf shots.

One thought at a time

Jack Nicklaus always used to say that he had one swing thought per day. No more than one and never nothing at all – just one simple thought that he took from the practice ground to the 1st tee with him. However he played, he would carry that swing thought

Even if it's only something very straightforward, like maintaining a smooth rhythm into your downswing as I'm doing here, it is still vital to have one key swing thought.

with him for the entire round. This is good advice. One of the problems I think all golfers have from time to time – and I include professionals – is having too much on their mind when they stand over the ball. It's often referred to as 'paralysis by analysis' and that about sums it up perfectly. You just can't make a free-flowing swing if your mind is cluttered, trying to piece together 15 different key moves. If anyone is gifted enough to cope with more than one swing thought, it is big Jack, and even he feels one is enough. So, take a leaf out of Nicklaus's book. Try to make time to hit balls before your round and, as you do, identify one key thought or move to help promote the smooth-running of your swing.

Your swing isn't going to feel the same every day, so your swing thought isn't always going to be the same, either. But it's usually possible to focus on one thing, something that feels right on the day – it might be the tempo of your takeaway or the change of direction. But once you decide on your 'thought of the day', stick with it.

Sweep away a second ball

To promote a wide, low-to-the-ground takeaway, imagine there is a second golf ball sitting 12in (30cm) behind the object ball, on exactly the same line. Address the shot and, as you start your takeaway, try to imagine that the clubhead sweeps the second ball away from the target. The clubhead will travel low to the ground, your wrists won't hinge too early and you'll create a wide arc in your backswing which is bound to help you hit the ball further. Simple but effective, just like so many of the best tips.

Stand your ground

I can't think of any professional golfers who don't 'stand their ground' in the followthrough. By that I mean that they hold their finish position, pretty much until the ball lands, striking the kind of pose in which you see me earlier.

As you will have already gathered, I'm a great believer in the benefits of a balanced, poised finish. It's the sign of a golfer who swings with control. No forcing the shot, no loss of balance, just a comfortable swing. So always try to finish like this. It will have a calming influence on your entire golf swing – start to finish – and I believe that will improve both the consistency and accuracy of your shots.

IRON PLAY

Make the same swing and let the clubs do the work

One of the best, and most frequent, compliments that I receive about my golf game is how my rhythm stays exactly the same for every club in the bag. "Ernie, whether it's a driver or a 9-iron, your rhythm and tempo never change," is the common remark. That's nice to hear, but it's not something that happens by accident. It's something I work on a great deal, and I would say that most of the poor shots that I hit arise from bad rhythm. The shape of my swing doesn't necessarily deteriorate, it's my rhythm that deserts me, and that can be expensive.

My drive on the par-5 13th at Augusta during the 1994 US Masters continues to be a painful reminder of this fact. I was in contention, just a few shots off the pace, and looking to pick up shots down the closing stretch – particularly on the par-5s, my speciality holes. But I got too quick with my drive, I snatched the club a bit from the top, and pull-hooked the ball into the magnolias and made bogey. That one lapse in my natural rhythm cost me a chance of winning the tournament – like I say, very expensive!

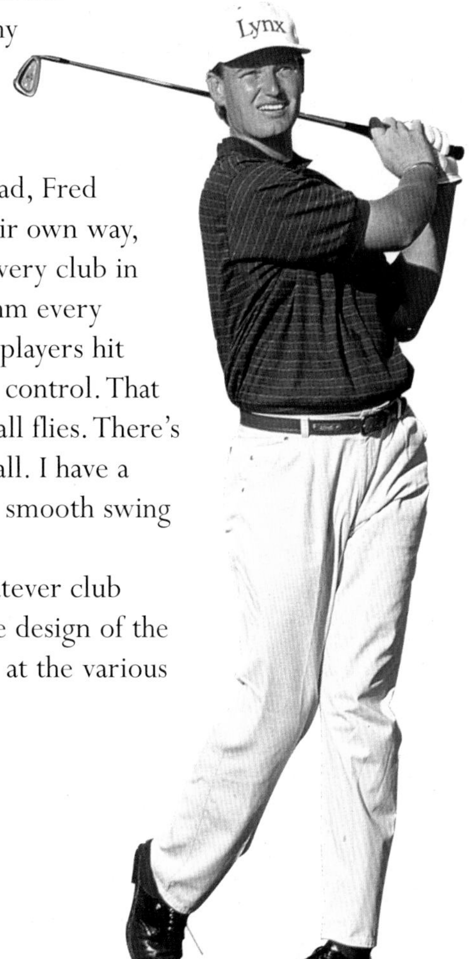

So, rhythm is crucial to me, just as it is with some other great players such as Sam Snead, Fred Couples, Nick Faldo and Payne Stewart. In their own way, and with their own method, they each swing every club in the bag exactly the same – with the same rhythm every time. Whenever you watch me or any of these players hit iron shots, look how the swing is always under control. That is what enables all of us to know how far the ball flies. There's no guess-work involved and no muscling the ball. I have a caddie to tell me the yardage and I just make a smooth swing and let the club do the work.

That's the first key to good iron play – whatever club you're hitting, make the same swing and let the design of the club do the hard work for you. Now, let's look at the various other factors involved in iron play.

Accuracy and distance

One of the essential keys to good iron play is distance control. Controlling accuracy and distance really is what it's all about. You might think that this is stating the obvious, but very few of the amateurs who I play with actually seem to put this statement into practice. A lot of the time they're hitting the ball too hard, taking too little club and over-powering the shot, all of which costs them accuracy and consistency.

If that sounds familiar to you, I think this stems from not having the confidence to judge how far you hit the ball with every iron club in the bag. There's always that doubt "have I got the right iron?" and usually it's too little club in the player's hand rather than too much. The result? Brute force and muscle-power take over, and that leads to inconsistency. The first thing to understand, then, is that each club is designed to hit the ball a certain distance. Again, that sounds obvious, but this still means that you have to find out what your own individual yardages are. The only place you can find this information is on the practice ground, hitting, if possible, the same type golf ball that you would in a round of golf. I'm afraid those soft balls at the driving range are not ideal for giving you an accurate idea of the distance your shots fly. So, set aside an afternoon, preferably on a calm day with little wind, and take every iron club to the range. Warm-up first and then work through the bag, hitting roughly 20 balls with each club. Keep a nice, even tempo and don't force your shots. Swing within yourself. Then pace out the distance to the main cluster of balls that you've hit.

Just by knowing how far you hit the ball, you'll knock shots off your score.

Ignore the freak long ones (and the duffed short ones) and concentrate on that main bunch. That's your average for that club, so write it down. Repeat this process with every club. With the short irons, where your shots will be pitching on the green, don't allow for much run on the ball when calculating the distance your shots fly. With the long irons, include any run that you get, but again, try to work out an average total distance.

On the course

Obviously when you're on the course, lots of other factors come into play, such as wind speed and direction, uphill or downhill terrain and soft or hard ground conditions. Golf isn't an exact science, after all. But if you have a base figure to work from, say on a still day it's 145yds (130m) with your 7-iron, you can at least make an educated guess. In time, this will give you the confidence to trust your judgement and that's bound to free-up your swing and help you play a better, more positive shot.

The other thing to remember, and this really is the most important part and something that a huge number of club golfers misunderstand, is that you don't have to change your swing to suit the different iron clubs. In all honesty, if you can hit one club in the bag nice and solidly, then you can hit any other club in the bag. Again, this might sound as though I'm over-simplifying the game of golf, but you really don't need to make any great conscious effort to swing them any differently. It is the design and make-up of the clubs themselves which determines how you should set up to the ball, and that then takes care of everything else as far as the swing is concerned. As I say, you don't need to consciously change a thing.

If you're like the majority of club golfers, this news is going to probably come as something of a surprise. Maybe even a bit of a shock. So let's grab three clubs in the range – a 2-iron, 6-iron and 9-iron – and I'll demonstrate exactly what I mean.

Take a leaf out of my book and develop the ability to control the distance of each iron club.

2-iron

A lethal weapon in the right hands

Here we are then with the 2-iron, one of my favourite clubs in the bag. In contrast, judging by what I mostly see in pro-ams, a lot of you are going to be thinking that this club is your worst nightmare. A lot of you guys probably don't even own one, let alone carry one around the golf course with you. Keep reading, though. For one thing, a 2-iron isn't a nightmare club; it really can be a useful weapon put in the right hands and, in any case, it isn't as difficult to hit as you might expect. Take into account that what I'm saying and demonstrating here can just as easily be applied to any of the longer clubs, from a 3-wood to a 1-iron or 3-iron. And I bet you carry at least one of those clubs, probably two of them – so this section should help you enormously.

Getting down to the bare essentials, the key to hitting good long iron shots is sweeping the ball away, rather like you should with a driver. There are certain factors both in your set-up and your swing, which determine whether you sweep the ball away and hit a good shot, or chop down too steeply and make a complete mess of your score, not to mention the golf course. Let's start by taking a look at these factors, which have such a huge influence on the nature of impact with your long irons.

GETTING YOUR POSTURE RIGHT

The most obvious thing about a 2-iron (apart from the lack of loft, which I'll come to shortly) is the length of the shaft. This, of course, affects how far you stand from the ball. This is an easy point to establish – if you get your posture right, remember the drill I showed you back on pages 24 and 25, you will automatically be standing the correct distance from the ball. And with good posture, this will help lead to the correct shape and plane of swing. I'll show you the comparisons between the different length irons at the end of this chapter, but essentially this means that your swing will be more rounded with the longer clubs, which promotes a more shallow angle of attack and a sweeping ball-strike.

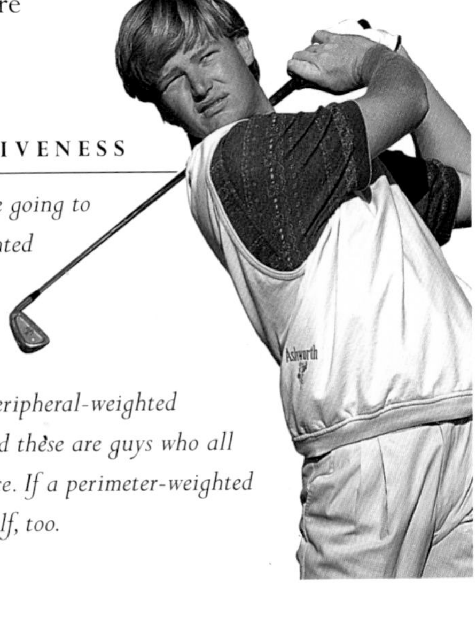

KEY TIP LONG IRON FORGIVENESS

Even if you prefer the look and feel of bladed irons, I think that if you're going to carry a 1- or 2-iron, then it's a good idea to make it a peripheral-weighted club. They're just that little bit more forgiving – and when you're teeing off, which you often will be with one of these long irons, then it's good to have that built-in forgiveness. If you were to peer into the golf bags at a professional event, you'd see a lot of the players using a peripheral-weighted 1-iron, even though as I say a lot of them carry blades. And bear in mind these are guys who all hit the ball very solidly and consistently out of the middle of the clubface. If a perimeter-weighted 1- or 2-iron is good enough for them, then it has to be good for your golf, too.

MEMORABLE SHOTS
THE 1994 GENE SARAZEN WORLD OPEN, CHATEAU ELAN, GEORGIA

As I've already mentioned, I have always thought that my long iron play is one of my biggest strengths. Of all the shots I've struck with these clubs, though, nothing so far can compare with the 3-iron I hit to the par-5 14th in the final round at the 1994 Gene Sarazen World Open. It was one of the purest shots I've ever struck.

The hole was a slight dogleg, just over 500yds (450m), and playing into the slightest of breezes. I hit a reasonable drive, but the ball finished in the left half of the fairway. That wasn't the best side to come in from, because there were some trees blocking a direct line to the flag. However, one of the advantages of long irons is that the straight face makes it easier to shape the ball through the air, so a shot to the green was definitely on. My caddie Ricky told me I had 240yds (219m) to the flag. We both agreed that a 3-iron was perfect, but I had to really hit it 'on the button'. My swing was feeling so good, though, I didn't have any doubts at all. I just felt, OK let's go for it.

I aimed a little right of the flag, closed the clubface a fraction and put the ball back in my stance. Then I took the club away nice and smooth, low to the ground, and concentrated on releasing the clubhead freely through the ball. I hit it right on the button – absolutely flush. The ball took just the right amount of swerve, pitched on the green and ran up to within 6ft (2m) of the hole.

POSITIONING THE BALL

The second part is ball position. It's another of those tedious, boring subjects that no club golfer wants to address. But I tell you again, if your ball position is bad you will never, and I mean never, hit good long iron shots. You just can't do it. To promote a sweeping action through the hitting area, you have to position the ball forward in your stance. As with the driver, opposite, or just inside, your left heel is the place –there's no room for compromise here. Further forward than that and you'll hit it on the up, or be reaching for the ball, which is awful. Any further back than that and you'll be too cramped in the downswing and hitting too steeply down, which isn't going to do you any favours, either.

Now, what about the loft, or lack of it? How do you deal with that? Well, you don't have to deal with it. If you do what I've just told you – in other words, establish a good posture and ball position – you've got all the loft you need to hit a good iron shot. You don't have to mess around trying to scoop or lift the ball into the air with a meddling hand action. Just set up solidly and swing smoothly. No swing changes are necessary and you don't have to hit the ball any harder; just maintain your natural rhythm and tempo.

Finally, look carefully at the sequence over the next eight pages of me hitting a 2-iron. As I've said, one of my biggest strengths as a golfer is my long iron play, and basically it all stems from the fundamentals I described in the last chapter. There's no magic formula to hitting these clubs – but it's not rocket science, either – so forget your fear of long irons. No one is born incapable of hitting these clubs. But you do have to accept that the fundamentals are essential to hitting these shots 'on the button'.

Get set at address

Note how my hands are over the ball and that my grip is perfectly neutral. You should make every effort to emulate that position, with your weight favouring your right side just a fraction. You should also feel a little tension in the tops of your thigh muscles with your knees nicely flexed. And remember, keep that ball up around your left heel.

The clubhead travels wide and slow

It is vital for you to establish a smooth tempo from the word go as it will set the pattern for your entire swing. Remember to maintain a constant, secure grip pressure, and try to think 'all arms' as you sweep the clubhead away from the ball. Even this early in the swing, you can see my left wrist starting to rotate, keeping the clubface square to the path of my swing.

Let your wrists hinge naturally

One of the advantages of a good grip is that your wrists are encouraged to hinge naturally, just as mine have here. Also allow your left hip and knee to work in towards the ball as your weight flows over on to your right foot. I like to consciously feel myself swinging slowly through my backswing – I think that's a good feeling for you to have, too.

Load up the power in your backswing

Now is the time time to coil your upper body as much as possible – this is where you generate your power. For the latter part of the backswing, try to sense that your body-weight is supported over your still-flexed right knee. Look how I have created room to turn my left shoulder under my chin. You can't hit solid golf shots if you don't do that.

Change down into power-drive

As you initiate the downswing, sense the gap widening between your left shoulder and your chin. At the same time, retain the angle in your left wrist as you bring the club down, just like I'm doing here. Above all, keep the rhythm of your downswing smooth – there is no point snatching the club down too aggressively; you don't hit the ball from here.

Impact – right on the button

Feel that most of your weight is supported over your left foot; your body open in relation to the target line. Try to condition yourself not to hit at the ball – think merely of the clubhead collecting the ball on its journey through impact. Get a little bit reckless and release the clubhead freely down the target line. There is little benefit in guiding the ball.

Fire your right shoulder past your chin

Just as you turn your left shoulder under your chin in the backswing, your right shoulder works under in the throughswing. You can see from the position of my hands how freely I've released the club. So really roll your right hand over your left through impact. The movement of my upper body is only now bringing my head up.

Hold your finish and watch it fly

As you move into the followthrough, try to avoid the strain of arching your lower spine by ensuring that your right shoulder finishes over your left foot as I'm doing here. A balanced followthrough is the trademark of a good player, so make it your trademark, too. There's no better feeling than nailing a long iron into the heart of a distant green, so enjoy the view!

The 6-iron

Improving your mid-iron accuracy

Here we move into the mid-iron range, specifically with a 6-iron. Admittedly, this isn't the sort of club that strikes fear into the hearts of golfers, like a long iron might, but in my opinion it's still a problem club in that most golfers aren't as accurate with it as they should be. Both in terms of line and length, there just isn't the necessary consistency or sharpness that I feel should be there.

If that's you, I'm sure you'd like to change your mid-iron play for the better. First of all, let's make one point very clear – you shouldn't sweep the ball away with your mid-irons. A slightly descending angle of attack is necessary to produce really crisp 6-iron shots, ideally leading to a strong, penetrating trajectory, the sort of flight that you see me and most other professionals hit. So that's your goal with this club: to generate a better flight, and with that, improve your accuracy and ability to judge the distance the ball flies through the air.

SUBTLE ADJUSTMENTS FOR THE MID-IRONS

First of all, let's look at the actual physical differences in the clubs themselves. The 6-iron is shorter than a 2-iron by some 2in (5cm), which means that you have to stand closer to the ball and bend more from the hips. As I said earlier, the design of the club determines the nature of your address position, not the other way round. All of which means that your swing will automatically be a little more upright than it is with a long iron. I'll say it again, you don't have to consciously try to make your swing more upright. Providing your posture is correct at address, it will happen. It's only natural. Feel that you keep your swing the same and let the club do the work.

This change in the shape of your swing, combined with the relatively short shaft of a 6-iron, leads to a slightly steeper angle of attack. And this is where ball position comes into the equation. If you were to put the ball opposite your left heel as you do with the 2-iron, the clubhead would have a tendency to make contact with the ground before the ball. Put more painfully, you'd 'dunch' your shots. With the ball too far back in your stance, the chances are you'll skull the ball. That's going to hurt your score and, if you use balata-covered golf balls, your wallet, too. So make absolutely sure that your ball position is spot-on. A useful rule of thumb is to start with the ball opposite your left heel for the driver and long irons, then move it back towards the centre of your stance by half-an-inch per iron club.

Now you're in great shape to hit some solid mid-iron shots. The combination of these address-factors helps produce the ideal shaped swing for the particular club, which leads to crisp ball-then-turf contact and a strong flight. Introduce these into your swing, like I have done on the following pages, and you will have more of a chance of developing the 'strong' ball-flight that is a feature of 99% of good players' golf shots.

KEY TIP KEEP A CONSTANT SPINE ANGLE

As I've touched upon over the last few pages, there are three main ingredients to hitting your iron shots with an impressive ball-flight – something every golfer wants to do. The clubface has to be square to the target line when it meets the ball. It also has to be travelling on the correct path; one that corresponds with the target line. And to finish off, it has to be travelling on the correct angle of attack.

To achieve all of this, your spine angle has to remain constant from address at least until impact and just beyond. You can't afford to be sliding from side to side too much, or moving up and down in the swing as that will upset all three of the key ingredients, and probably leave a nasty taste in your mouth to boot!

Now I know as well as you do that it's hard to focus on your spine angle while you're swinging the club. You can't actually see your own swing – you can only feel it. However, let me explain to you some of my key thoughts and feelings about how you can make sure that your spine angle does stay the same from address to impact. Hopefully this will make the difference.

First, of course, you have to make absolutely sure that your spine is at the correct angle to start with. If it's not, then you're really fighting an uphill battle from the word 'go'. As a guide to establishing the correct spine angle, check that the middle of your right shoulder is roughly level with the outside of your right knee. That's ideal, whether you're 6ft 3in (1.9m) like me, or indeed any other height you may care to think of. You don't want your spine to be too straight at address, or you're going to have to dip down into the ball as you approach impact; or too bent over, which will mean you have to come up into impact in order to make good contact with the ball.

Try to imagine your spine as a central column, with your upper body rotating around it. That's the essence of maintaining a constant spine angle. You don't want to be wavering too much from side to side and certainly not moving up and down. The spine stays fixed from the moment you address the ball to the moment it fizzes into the distance.

The only time your spine angle should change is when your upper body becomes more upright to ease the pressure on your lower back as you swing through to a balanced followthrough. So, get your spine angle correct and you're really in business.

Set the correct spine angle.

And keep that angle constant...

...at least until impact.

Bring your posture into play

Make your stance slightly narrower than for a long-iron and check that the ball is approximately 2in (5cm) inside your left heel. Make sure your hips, shoulders and feet are parallel to, rather than aiming at, the target. Finally, try to feel as though the shaft is an extension of your left arm, forming a straight line down to the ball.

Avoid loose connections

Note here how the clubhead is outside the line of my hands, a tell-tale sign of the correct swing path. As you do this, your shoulders should just start to show the first signs of turning. Remember also that a one-piece takeaway is essential, so make sure you don't get too wristy, too early. That would almost certainly throw your swing out of sync.

The 3 o'clock position

This is where your arm should form a 90° angle with the shaft. Sense that while you're turning your back on the target, your head remains motionless. Also note how the butt of the shaft points midway between my toes and the ball – perfectly on plane.

Perfectly poised at the top

As you reach the top, your spine-angle and head-height should be exactly as they were at address. As you can see from my position looking down the target line, there is no 'light' showing between my knees – they are providing resistance as the upper body rotates. I am now in full control – poised and ready to swing the club down to the ball.

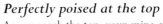

'Settle' and unwind

Think 'left knee first' as you settle your weight towards the target and start to unwind your upper body. Also keep your head behind the point of impact. If there is one key message in this transition from backswing to downswing, I think it is to keep everything smooth.

Make a good impact

As you swing down to impact, sense that you really 'zip' the clubhead through the ball. Listen to the sound of a crisp strike and store it in your mind. You will instinctively know when you make a crisp strike and this can be kept as a benchmark for all your shots.

After the moment of truth

If it helps you release the clubhead more freely, try to make the toe of the club pass the heel through impact, and roll your right hand over your left. Don't deliberately keep your head down – simply allow the momentum of your swing to lift it for you.

Study your pretty picture

Make it a habit of yours to hold your followthrough position until the ball lands...hopefully next to the pin. Show the spikes on your right foot and sense that most of your weight is supported over the outside of your left foot. One other thing: try to ensure that the buckle on the belt of your trousers faces the target. I always think that this shows you've really got 'through the ball'.

The 9-iron

All about accuracy and control

Now we're moving into the serious scoring range. With anything like a 9-iron in my hands, I'm looking to knock some approach shots 'stiff'. And really you should set your sights pretty high, too. This club is all about accuracy – it should never be thought of as just an 'anywhere on the green' club.

Obviously, how far you are physically capable of hitting a lofted iron is totally irrelevant. I could probably hit a 9-iron as much as 180yds (165m) if I really leant on it, but there's no point. I've got other clubs in the bag to hit the ball that far, which require a lot less effort. My nice, controlled 9-iron swing sends the ball between 130–140yds (119–128m) and that suits me just fine. Once I've worked out the yardage to the pin, I can then focus on making a smooth swing and knocking-out the flag-stick.

THE SWING STAYS THE SAME

Let's get down to it, then. Although we're dealing with another different club, the theme is still the same. And by now you're hopefully getting used to the idea that you don't need to change your swing to suit the various clubs in your golf bag. To hit crisp short-iron shots the clubhead has to meet the ball on a slightly descending angle of attack. You

KEY TIP KEEP THOSE GROOVES DIRT-FREE

Backspin is your reward for paying attention to the details of your set-up and making a good swing, but all that hard work will go to waste if the grooves on your clubface are clogged with dirt and grass. The ball may pitch on the green but you certainly won't get the action that you expected, or needed. And that will cost you strokes, guaranteed.

Always make sure your grooves are dirt-free, on all of your irons, but particularly the more lofted clubs. It needn't delay play, you can do it while you're walking up the fairway towards the green, and it isn't difficult – a wooden tee-peg does the job. Have a damp towel in your bag, too, to wipe the face clean. It's something that I would never go on to the golf course without – and neither would any other professional in the world. It means that every time you address the ball you can look down on a sparkling, shiny clubface. Personally, I like to see that. It gives me a little bit of a lift. It can have the same effect on you, too, and also ensure that your good shots create the backspin on the ball that you deserve. A just reward.

Clean grooves will help you impart lots of spin, but remember to clean them after each shot!

really can't sweep these shots away, you have to strike down and, once again, a good address position pre-sets these ideal impact factors.

For a start, because the 9-iron is almost 4in (10cm) shorter than a 2-iron, you're going to have to stand a lot closer to the ball. That's only natural. You have to bend more from the hips, too, which means your spine angle becomes flatter than for longer irons. This is the factor which most influences the shape of your swing – it automatically gets more upright. And it is this which leads to a steeper angle of attack. Once again, as with the 2-iron and 6-iron, your ball position has to coincide with this angle of attack. Get it right – in other words, somewhere around the middle of your stance – and you stand every chance of achieving crisp, ball-then-turf contact. If it's too far forward, or too far back, in your stance then you're going to have a really tough time making good contact.

Memorable Shots
1994 World Matchplay, Wentworth

A lot of very knowledgable people have said that my second-round match against Seve Ballesteros in the 1994 World Matchplay was one of the greatest in the tournament's illustrious history. During the match, you obviously don't have time to be thinking about things like that, but looking back, I guess it was pretty special. Seve made seven twos out of the eight par-3s we played, 13 birdies in all, and still lost!

But for all the fireworks, the highlight of the match for me was the eagle-two I made on the uphill 3rd. With a long, double-tiered green, the second shot in there is a pretty tough proposition. And when Seve hit his shot into 12ft (4m), it certainly didn't look any easier. I had 155yds (146m) to the pin, as I say slightly uphill, and I decided to go in with plenty of club, an 8-iron, to make sure I didn't leave the ball short.

What happened then was beyond even my expectations. The ball covered the flag all the way – one of those gorgeous shots that never leaves the pin. I knew it was going to finish close, but I didn't expect it to hop into the hole for an eagle-two. Definitely a shot to savour and remember for many years. Oh, and I birdied it the next day, too. Five shots to play that hole twice, not a bad couple of days work.

If there's a lesson for the club golfer here, I think it's to understand the value of knowing how far you hit the ball with each club in the bag. This knowledge can give you so much extra confidence over the ball, and really free-up your swing.

Home in on the pin

As with all clubs in the bag, setting up to the ball correctly is a huge step towards hitting a good shot. I said earlier that the 9-iron requires a descending angle of attack, but you don't have to consciously hit down on the ball. Just set-up to the ball, think rhythm, swing smoothly, and the design of the golf club and length of shaft will take care of the rest for you. You'll hit crisp iron shots, you'll get a nice flight on the ball, and it will sit down on the green for you, hopefully next to the pin.

Like me, you'll soon develop the confidence to almost get 'cocky' with these lofted iron shots. I never dream of missing a green with a club like a 9-iron in my hands. I'm 'zeroed-in' on the pin – nothing else. That's the way you can be, too. You'll forget about the bunker on the right, or the bank to the left of the green, you'll just be thinking 'birdie'. That kind of attitude, just as much as a good technique, is what makes a good golf shot. So let's go for it!

Ball back, weight evenly spread

So here we are with the 9-iron, a club with serious pin-peppering potential. The key aspect of the address position with any lofted club is that you move the ball back in your stance to coincide with the steeper angle of attack – roughly four balls' width inside your left heel is ideal. Also sense that your weight is evenly spread on both feet.

Start smoothly

As with any shot in golf, your first move away from the ball sets a definite pattern for the entire swing. That's why it is essential to start your swing smoothly. It helps keep you co-ordinated, with everything moving away in unison – in my opinion, this is one of the real keys to consistent shot-making.

Left shoulder under the chin

As your arms continue to swing, simply turn your left shoulder under your chin, and keep the word 'rhythm' at the forefront of your mind. Looking at my position down the target line, you can see that the butt of the club is pointing to a spot on the ground mid-way between my toes and the ball – that's ideal. Also, really try to sense that your arms and body are working together.

Turn your back on the target

As I have mentioned with the other irons, you should complete your backswing by turning your back on the target, while allowing your weight to flow over towards your right side. One final thing about the backswing, the club should stop well short of horizontal when you are using a short-iron – if it doesn't, then you're sacrificing accuracy, guaranteed.

Smoothly does it on the way down

Short-irons are all about accuracy so don't go trying to force the shot. Make a smooth transition into your downswing and maintain a smooth, 'slow-motion' rhythm. I always like to think this – you don't want to be in a hurry to get that clubhead down to the ball, so give yourself time for everything to slot into place. Now you're in perfect shape to deliver the clubface square to the ball.

Contact is crisp and clean

One of the benefits of correct ball position is that when I swing the clubhead down, I don't have to make any compensations. It's ball first, then turf – perfect contact. All I'm really thinking about at this stage of the swing is: "Okay Ernie, keep your rhythm and smoothly accelerate the clubhead through impact". I suggest you keep your thoughts on a similar level.

Perfect balance through impact

I like these images because they're proof that my swing is perfectly under control through the ball – the one area of the swing where you can't get away with any flaw, however tiny it may be. My balance is good, everything's working together, and that really is how you should feel through impact. There's no need to be too aggressive, just keep everything smooth.

Followthrough reflects controlled swing

Here's another position which, if everyone concentrated on swinging through to, would improve their game enormously. There's no way I could go at the ball too aggressively and still finish the swing like this. Even before you address the ball, make it your goal to finish as balanced as possible. You'll feel that you have control over the clubhead – and that's where accuracy comes from.

In summary – comparing the three swings

Address: Note how much further I am from the ball with a 2-iron in my hands compared to the 9-iron. And look at the difference in my spine angle and overall posture – that's what determines the plane of my swing with each club. Remember, more rounded for the long clubs and slightly more upright for the short irons. From the face-on angle you can see that the ball is some 3in (15cm) further back in my stance with the 9-iron than it is with the 2-iron. Also my feet are further apart with the 2-iron to provide a stable base to support what will be a longer, more powerful swing.

2-iron

6-iron

9-iron

Top of backswing: Once again, slightly different positions, but in each case there's no conscious effort on my part to change the swing. See how the 9-iron doesn't get near parallel at the top of the backswing and is on a relatively upright plane – all just as it should be. Remember, the long shaft of the 2-iron makes me stand further from the ball and that's what contributes to a more rounded top-of-the-backswing position. The club also reaches horizontal. You can see that the shaft runs along a line parallel with the target line, and the clubface matches the angle of my left forearm.

2-iron

6-iron

9-iron

Impact: Here we have three good positions at impact, and really not a great deal of difference between them. In each case, my left side has cleared out of the way, with my hips, shoulders and upper body all open to the target line. This creates all the room I need to swing the club freely and powerfully into the back of the ball. I couldn't do that if my body didn't behave correctly. You can see from the amount of turf taken exactly what my angle of attack is. A downward hit with the 9-iron, where more of a divot is taken after the ball; more of a sweeping action with the 2-iron, where I've merely shaved the tops of the grass through impact; and the 6-iron, of course, somewhere in between – a slightly descending blow being the ideal contact for a crisp mid-iron shot.

2-iron

6-iron

9-iron

Followthrough: Some things never change. No matter what club I'm hitting, I always finish in perfect balance, as you can see here. That's something you should strive to achieve, also. It's the sign of a well-controlled, classic swing. The mark of a good player. Remember, keep the swing the same and let the club do the work for you. That is what it's designed to do.

2-iron

6-iron

9-iron

The Long Bunker Shot

An object lesson in ball-striking

A feature of all good golfers is the quality of their ball-striking. On a decent lie, nothing gets between the clubface and the ball – contact is crisp and clean. That's where the backspin comes from on my short irons, and that's where I get the penetration with my long irons. It's ball, then turf. Not the other way round.

If your ball-striking isn't quite spot-on, you can probably just about get away with it on most lies. There is one exception, though, and that's the long bunker shot. For anyone who thinks they're hitting the ball pretty well, these shots can be a humbling experience. You only have to catch a few too many grains of sand before impact and the ball travels half the distance you expect it to.

By practising the points I'm about to show you, however, you can start to hit the ball crisply and cleanly from the sand. You can then transfer those thoughts and sensations on to grass, achieving much better contact. And that's going to make a huge difference to the flight of your iron shots. I would recommend hitting long bunker shots as a regular part of your practice routine. Sand is very unforgiving so you'll know how well you are performing, by the way the ball flies.

There are several other reasons why practising out of sand is good for your golf swing, though. It's a great way to build perfect rhythm. Just stand in the sand, don't waggle your feet down too deeply, and make some smooth swings. You can't go at the ball too aggressively from the top because you'll lose your footing, so you're training a smoother transition from the top of the backswing to the start of the downswing.

It's also beneficial for those of you who have a tendency to slide your legs or jump at the ball too fiercely. Because you don't have such a secure footing as you would have on grass, you've got to stay steady on your feet, thereby 'quietening' your leg action.

So don't look at bunkers purely from a negative point of view. Use them to improve your golf game. You may find it a bit of a shock at first – your ball-striking might not be as good as you thought – but keep at it. In the long term it really will improve your golf swing.

Address determines quality of impact

I set up to this shot mostly like any other regular iron shot and I suggest you do, too. The only minor changes that you need to make are placing the ball a fraction further forward in your stance to encourage a sweeping angle of attack; and choking down on the grip at least one inch to promote clean contact. Don't bury your feet too far down in the sand (I'll explain exactly why a little further on in the sequence) and, obviously, hover the clubhead behind the ball. Now you're all set to hit a good, clean, long-range bunker shot. One final thing before you start the swing. I suggest you take one extra club from sand. So if you would normally hit a 6-iron from the same distance out on the fairway, go with your 5-iron from a bunker. Providing, of course, that gives you enough loft to clear the front lip.

Set-off the chain reaction

By now you'll know how important I believe the takeaway is to the success of all your golf shots. So important, in fact, that if you make a bad first move away from the ball, then I can't see any possible way you can play consistently good golf. With a shot such as the long bunker shot, your margin for error is even smaller, so it's critical that you keep everything moving in unison – nice and smoothly, too. As you take the club back, wide and slow, feel the whole of your left side being pulled in towards the ball.

Leg action must be 'quiet'

From a smooth start, you can just go ahead and make your regular backswing. Turn your left shoulder under your chin, continue to transfer your weight over a flexed right knee and keep a nice even tempo. The only slightly different sensation that I want you to concentrate on here is keeping your leg action 'quiet'. By that I mean don't allow your legs to bend and buckle all over the place – keep them nice and steady, supporting the turning motion of your upper body.

Keep the club 'in the groove'

You have to try to make your backswing just a fraction shorter than you might for a regular iron shot with this club. So really sense that you stop the club short of the horizontal. For a shot such as this, where impact needs to be precise, I think this is a useful image to have in mind. It helps you give your swing a compact, controlled feel to it. One thing I also want you to take note of here is my spine angle. See how it is exactly the same at the top of the backswing as it was at address. And it will stay that way until the ball is dispatched on its way.

Eye the back of the ball

In the downswing, keep your rhythm smooth and don't try to force the shot. Just concentrate on keeping everything nice and controlled with your eyes focussed on the back of the ball. You can see from the photograph on the right how the movement of my body unwinding drops the club down on ideal plane from which to attack the ball. And again, see how my spine angle is exactly the same as it was at address. I've maintained my original height throughout my swing. The one message I want you to take from this is how by using your body correctly, all the other elements of the swing slot more easily into place. If your body is doing all the wrong things, though, you'll always be making the game more difficult.

Concentrate on crisp contact

As I've said, sand is a lot more unforgiving than grass. If you catch the shot even a little heavy it will take a huge chunk of distance off the shot. Concentrate on clipping the ball away cleanly – almost as though you were sweeping the ball off a tee-peg. That's why I think the ball is best placed somewhere around opposite your left heel, which is obviously further forward than it would be for a regular mid-iron shot. This position helps promote a more shallow angle of attack, which encourages a sweeping motion and prevents the clubhead digging too deeply into the sand.

Control through the ball

Through impact, you can see that there's no great effort on my part to lift the ball into the air, or guide it in the right direction. It's just a case of me having chosen a lofted enough club to clear the front lip, and then simply trusting my swing. And that's really the stage that you have to get to. You have to commit yourself 100% through the hitting zone. Make your decision about the shot you're going to hit and stick with it. It's the only way to play these 'scary' shots.

Maintain your balance...and your footing

The reason I said earlier you shouldn't bury your feet too far into the sand is that it encourages you to swing more smoothly. See here how the sand is relatively undisturbed. I haven't been lurching from side to side, digging great troughs in the sand. My leg action has stayed pretty quiet – steady from the waist down – my balance and clubhead control perfect from start to finish. I think of you do bury your feet down deeply, though, it almost gives you too much of a secure footing. I know that sounds strange, but in my view this allows you licence to be too aggressive. And that is when you start to put yourself at risk of taking far too much sand. So, keep your footing and your balance, all the way to a perfect finish, and you'll hit far more consistent shots from the sand.

PITCHING

Not just another full swing

In this section I'm going to talk to you about a stroke which I see played badly as much as any other shot in golf – the pitch shot. Now, I can tell you that this is a pretty serious shot to get wrong. Instead of setting up birdie opportunities, you'll be missing greens and too often struggling to make par.

Not only will that start to wear you down but it will also place a huge amount of pressure on your chipping and putting. So as well as failing to make birdies, you will also be making plenty of bogeys from nowhere. Add all these factors together and you're looking at a potential eight, maybe even ten-shot, shift in one single round of golf – something we could all do without!

Like all professionals, I regard myself as a pretty good pitcher of the ball. I can even be 'red-hot' sometimes – and those are the days when the course records can go. With that in mind, let me show you what I feel are the most important ingredients to a good pitching action, together with why I think a lot of club golfers are bad in this area.

Where to begin

Let's get the mistakes out of the way to start with. I guess one of the main areas of confusion here is that there are a lot of misconceptions connected with pitching. Lots of golfers think it's just like every other full shot, and that's the first mistake. Others will do anything they can to muscle a pitching-wedge 150yds (137m) on to the green – almost as though hitting as little club as possible makes it a better shot. Another mistake.

Pitching isn't just another full shot. You need to make a few subtle changes at address, which then have an influence on the shape of your swing, to be a good pitcher of the ball. And you certainly don't need to muscle the ball. Accuracy, control and judgement of distance are the three key elements. So let's get down to technique and start the job of turning you into a better pitcher.

Don't force your pitch shots – swing within yourself and stay in control.

KEY TIP GET ARMED FOR THE JOB

I carry three wedges and I would say there's hardly a professional playing the game today who doesn't do exactly the same. That's another example you should follow; I don't care how far you hit the ball or how good you think your short game is, you need three wedges – it's as simple as that. From 100yds (90m) in, that's where you make your score, it's where you do all your work. Pitching the ball close, chipping and putting to make par, conjuring-up sand-saves from everywhere – to play these shots as well as you possibly can, you need to be properly armed for the job.

The three wedges that I carry have lofts of 52°, 56° and 60°, and I know exactly how far I hit the ball with each of them. Once I've taken into account the firmness of the putting surface, and any wind that might affect the flight of the ball, this gives me the confidence to make a free swing, knowing exactly how far the ball will carry through the air. That's a huge asset, because it removes any doubt from my mind. I'm not second-guessing or trying to guide the ball. My caddie gives me the yardage and I immediately know what swing to put on the ball.

That's the kind of approach you have to adopt for pitching. It should be a precise business – not a case of hit and hope. So arm yourself with three wedges and learn how far you comfortably hit each one. You'll start to set up far more birdie opportunities and make many more up-and-downs from around the green to save par.

MEMORABLE SHOTS
THE 1995 BUICK CLASSIC, WESTCHESTER

If you were to look back on some of your best rounds – days when you've beaten your handicap by a country mile, won the monthly medal by a street, or dispatched an opponent for an early bath in a matchplay final – often it's one shot early in the round that triggers-off a purple patch. It's hard to put your finger on the exact feeling, but something seems to 'click'.

That's just what happened to me at the 1995 Buick Classic at Westchester. I'd had a poor third round which had left me too many shots off the lead for comfort. Starting my final round, I knew I had to make something happen pretty quickly. After an okay drive on the 3rd, I had exactly 133yds (122m) to the flag. Using a pitching-wedge, I hit it real solid, and in it rolled for an eagle-two. That was the start of an eagle-birdie-birdie run and by then I was really fired-up. Unfortunately, it just wasn't enough to overhaul the winner, Vijay Singh, but that's besides the point – if you get a break early in a round, think positive and really go for it. Believe me, it could well be your day.

Set-up open to the target

The first, and most important, aspect of your address position for pitching is adopting a slightly open stance. It needn't be anything too severe, just enough so as your feet and hips are aligned maybe 15ft (5m) left of parallel to the target – that's ideal.

This encourages a slightly more upright backswing, perfect for pitching, and keeps your hip-turn in check, thus helping to create some resistance as you rotate your upper body in the backswing. More importantly, it gives your left side a 'head start' in the downswing (I'll explain that in more detail when we come to it). So, set up slightly open as I am here. It'll 'quieten' your lower body action, which is a good thing in itself, and give you a better opportunity to clear that left side for impact.

Another point to check is that your ball position is around the centre of your stance. This encourages the clubhead to meet the ball cleanly, on a slightly descending angle of attack. Also check that the shaft of the club and your left arm form virtually a straight line down to the ball. Your weight should be evenly distributed on both feet.

Stay connected in the backswing

One of the biggest mistakes that I see golfers make when they're hitting short pitch shots is that they get too wristy in the early part of the takeaway. I don't know why they feel they have to do this, but the moment they do, it causes a loss of co-ordination and, inevitably, major problems in judging both line and length. Which is how you miss greens.

So just for a second I want you to think back to the section on the full swing and, in particular, my key thought for the takeaway. 'All arms' is what I said then, and it applies just as much here with the pitching-wedge as it did then with the driver. You have to have width in your swing, whether you're hitting the ball 300yds (274m) or 100yds (92m), and to achieve that your swing has to start in one-piece.

Stand in the mirror and copy this position of me here, rehearsing it over and over again. Make sure it has all the correct elements: the arms sweeping the club away from the ball; the left shoulder following suit; the wrists passive; the clubhead travelling low to the ground; the clubface square to the path of your swing and the knees nicely flexed. That's what I would call an impressive start to your swing and it will make life a lot easier from here on.

Set the club on the correct plane

From a good, one-piece takeaway you are then ideally positioned to set the club on the correct plane in the backswing. This involves turning your upper body and hingeing your wrists, almost to their fullest extent, so that the shaft of the club and your left forearm form a 90-degree angle. You can tell if you've performed this correctly by looking back at your reflection in a mirror, so that you see yourself side-on as I am here. With your left arm horizontal to the ground, the butt-end of the club should point at a spot on the ground between the ball and your toes. If that's the case, congratulations, you're on plane.

I don't want you to tie yourself in knots over this. All you really should be thinking is nothing more than a 'one-two' movement: one-piece takeaway and then set. Swing thoughts such as this are good for your practice sessions. They help keep you on the right track and, at the same time, build that all-important muscle memory which hopefully sticks with you out on the golf course.

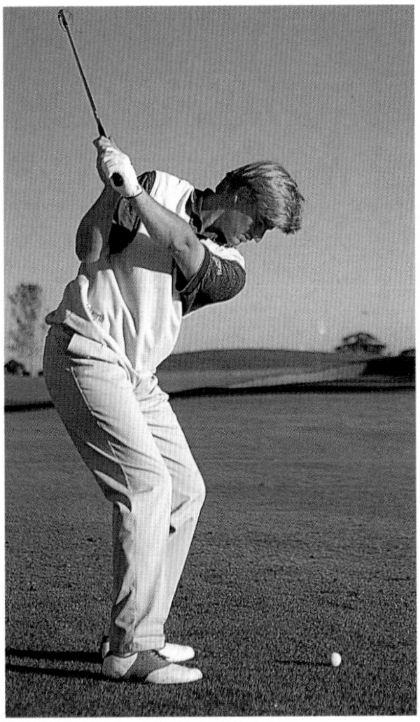

Swing to a tidy top-of-the-backswing position

To get to the top of your backswing, all you need to feel is that you rotate your upper body and swing the club all the way to the top. It's as simple as that. The open alignment should help curb the movement of your lower body and prevent you turning your right side too far behind the ball. This added element of resistance reduces your backswing to a tidy, three-quarter position, just as you can see here. The position of the club shouldn't feel lose at the top – you should 'know where it is'.

A word of warning, though. Despite the shorter swing, you still need to transfer your weight correctly. Sense that you load your weight into your right side. That will help guard against any potentially disastrous leaning onto your left foot in the backswing. Feel your left shoulder moving 'around' rather than 'down'. This encourages a good turn, and again, prevents you reverse pivoting in the backswing.

Make the transition a good one

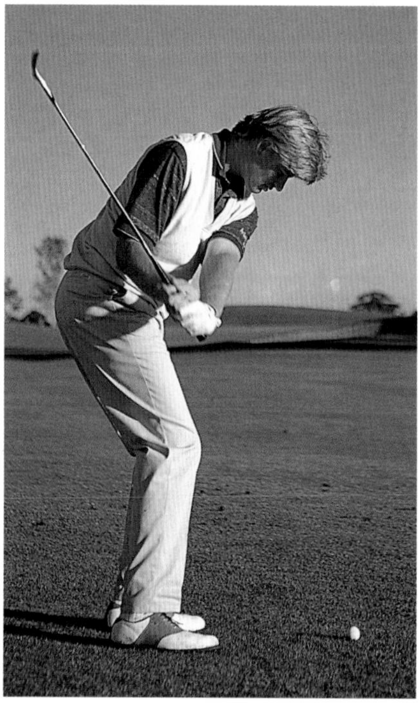

Now is the time to look at the benefits of that open stance in even more detail. Because the swing is relatively short (the shaft of the club should stop well short of horizontal at the top, remember) your body has less time to turn out of the way in the downswing. Having opened your stance, though, you've made it a lot easier to clear your left side. As I said a little earlier, you're giving your left side a head start, which is exactly what you need.

Look at me here, and again, grab a club and copy the positions I'm demonstrating. As I bring the club down on the correct path, you can see that my left side is already moving out of the way, giving me all the room I need to swing the club freely through the ball. Let me stress that word 'freely' again, because it's important. If you set up square to the target with your pitching-wedge, you'll get 'stuck' in the downswing. There's no way you can get your left side out of the way soon enough. In other words, there's no room for you to swing the club freely, down and through impact. And that's where you start having problems, because it severely restricts your ability to strike the ball solidly. You'll end up just scooping at the ball.

Strike the ball squarely and solidly

As your left side clears, your arms have plenty of room to deliver the clubhead squarely to the ball, on the correct path and on a slightly descending angle of attack. You don't have to consciously hit down on the ball – you'll probably hit the shot heavy if you do that. Just trust your swing and let it happen.

The clubface (which is square, courtesy of a good grip) meets the ball first, then the turf, taking the customary divot – courtesy of good ball position. And the clubhead is travelling on the absolute ideal path for straight, accurate golf shots – courtesy of a good posture and alignment.

Note also how my weight is supported mainly on my front foot. My head is over the point of impact – I'm not leaning backwards trying to help the ball into the air, or lunging forwards trying to muscle the ball 160 yards (146m) through the air. I just swing smoothly, keep my rhythm and let the club do the work for me.

With practice, you'll also start to get that lovely, crisp ball-then-turf contact. You'll immediately feel the difference as the sensation of a really quality strike rises up through the clubhead, into your hands and arms.

Release the clubhead through impact

What you see here is me benefiting from the good work I did earlier in the swing – nothing more. I couldn't pose this for you – it's a position within motion. And that's all it should be for you, too.

From a good position just before impact, I've basically released the clubhead freely through the ball. And I think that is the key phrase – freely through the ball. You don't want to feel that you hit at the ball.

So if there is one swing thought that can help you at, what is, a fairly late stage of the swing, then it's to hit through the ball. I can't say much more, other than if you get yourself into this kind of position through impact, then your swing is taking shape very nicely indeed. You can be proud of yourself. And you'll see one heck of a difference, too. The trajectory will be much stronger, the ball fighting tooth and nail to hold it's line for you. And when it pitches on the green you'll get just the kind of response you want – one bounce and then plenty of check-spin to make it sit down next to the hole.

Show your spikes in the follow-through

Well again, there's no way you can get into a good followthrough position like this unless you do a lot of good work earlier in the swing. As with all shots, you should try to finish in perfect balance – and then hold it, just like you're posing for a photograph. Check that your weight is supported on your left foot; your right shoulder is over your left toe; the spikes on your right foot are in full view. Memorise this position and swing to it, every time.

Now you've got a better pitching action all round. And I'll tell you something, with good technique such as this, you can look forward to a lot of birdie putts and a lot of cheeky par-saves.

Ashworth

DEVELOPING YOUR OWN BEST RHYTHM

Your golf swing's best ally

Arnold Palmer once said that great rhythm can get a golfer out of jail, and he's absolutely right. Rhythm really can get you out of all kinds of trouble on a golf course – as long as it's good rhythm, that is. I should know because the rhythm in my golf swing is perhaps my greatest asset. Good rhythm makes my bad shots less bad – and my good shots even better. The same principle applies to everyone's golf game, including yours, and I tell you, if you can develop a good rhythm, your golf swing will have a friend for life.

The trouble is, that of all the different ingredients that go towards making up the ideal golf swing, probably the hardest thing to show in photographs is good, or indeed bad, rhythm. Moving images are really the only way of capturing it totally and perfectly.

Still, that's not to say I can't teach you an awful lot about the rhythm of my golf swing. In this section I'll tell you why good rhythm is so important to playing good golf and how you can find your own best rhythm for your swing. And just as importantly, I'll explain how you can then maintain that perfect rhythm when it matters most, under pressure, during a good competition round – when the 'heat is on'.

Determining your rhythm

The first thing you have to understand, however, is that what's good rhythm for one person is not necessarily good rhythm for you. That's why slow swingers sometimes don't like playing with fast swingers. Likewise, some fast swingers cannot bear to watch those with a slower tempo. The fact is, playing a full 18 holes with someone who swings at a completely different rhythm and tempo to you can, if you're not careful, upset your natural rhythm. It's almost as though you pick up their habits and you've got to make sure that doesn't happen to you in any way.

So, you know rhythm varies from one person to the next. But how do you find your best rhythm? Well, looking at both golfers on tour and amateur players, I

KEY TIP SWISH THE SHAFT TO REGAIN RHYTHM

Keeping a good rhythm at the range is easy – you're often hitting the same club for 20 or 30 shots, maybe more, and you kind of get into the groove. On the course, though, it's very easy to lose your rhythm. Things can upset you – one bad shot, a delay on a hole, strong winds, perhaps even doubt about what club to hit – and it can be very difficult to get your rhythm back.

Here's an exercise that I've seen many professionals doing in the middle of a round, and it's ideal for getting the rhythm back in your swing. It's one that is well worth trying. When you have a minute in between shots, then, grip the clubhead-end of your driver and swish it back and forth. Make your normal swing and try to focus on the sound of the shaft as you swing it down and through. Don't think about anything else – just listen to the 'whoosh' as you whip the shaft through where the ball would normally be. Make as many of these swings as you want to. Now flip the club back the correct way, adopt a nice, tension-free grip, and make some smooth practice swings, back and forth, almost lazily. Immediately, you should be more aware of the weight of the clubhead and more conscious of the pace of your swing. And that's the key. If you're in control of the pace of your swing again, you can get back that lost rhythm. Crisis over!

KEY TIP SWING AT A PERCENTAGE OF YOUR FULL POWER

When you drive your car to work, you don't go round corners like Nigel Mansell, do you? Well, at least I hope you don't, for the sake of your passengers! If you did approach bends at 130mph (208mph), I think it's pretty safe to say that you'd crash the car before too long.

Right now you're probably asking yourself what relevance this has to the game of golf. Well, I mention it because I'm always surprised to see club players trying to hit the ball as hard as John Daly. I mean, just because Mansell can control a car at full tilt, and Daly can control a golf club at full tilt, doesn't mean to say you can copy them. You have to find a 'level' that suits your ability. So next time you're on the practice ground, perform the following exercise. Grab 10 balls and hit shots with a mid-iron, trying to sense that you swing at 60% of full power with each shot. It may take a little getting used to, but that's the feeling I want you to have. After those 10 shots, make a mental note of how well you performed at that speed.

Now grab another 10 balls and hit shots swinging at what you feel is 70% of full power. Sense that you change up a gear, and again, see how solidly you perform and how accurate your shots are. Repeat the exercise at 80%, 90% and finally at what you feel is full power – 100%. My guess is that one of these 'speeds' will feel better than all of the others, producing shots that are purely struck, more accurate and more consistent. That is the feeling you should look to repeat over the course of 18 holes next time you play. In a sense, that is your speed limit. So stick to it. The wheels will come off less often, believe me.

often feel that the rhythm of someone's golf swing should reflect their personality. In other words, if you're a hyper-active, fast-talking, fast-walking kind of person then it's my guess that you'll be best off with a brisk rhythm to your golf swing. That's natural. Just like Tom Watson and Lanny Wadkins – they walk fast, think fast and swing the golf club pretty fast, too. The thing is, it's perfect rhythm for them. If they tried to swing slowly, neither of them would be as good a player.

Looking at the opposite end of the scale, if you're a laid-back, relaxed, slow-walking type of person, then your best rhythm will ideally be slower and more languid. Like me or, Fred Couples, for instance. We're both pretty laid back off the golf course – and both of us swing the club at a pretty slow, easy pace. It's completely different to Lanny Wadkins, but that, for us, is perfect rhythm. If Freddie and I tried to swing it as fast as Lanny, there probably wouldn't be a golf course in the world wide enough for us!

Now are you starting to get a feel for what I mean? The first and most important thing you have to do is decide what type of person you are. Laid-back, like me; or fast-talking, fast-walking, like Lanny. This shouldn't take too long or be too difficult and it gives you a basis upon which to develop the best rhythm for your golf swing. On top of that, I'm going to demonstrate for you a couple of drills and exercises that I think will help you find, and just as importantly maintain, a rhythm to suit your own golf swing.

Finding your own best rhythm – easy as 1, 2, 3

As I've said, finding the best rhythm for your swing is almost an instinctive thing. And if you feel that you're a laid-back type of person, then I think the method I'm about to demonstrate for you here will help you enormously. It's simple – as long as you can count to three you can do it! – but still don't make the mistake of thinking it's too simple. It is very effective and certainly it's something that I've found useful from time to time over the years.

Here's how it works. Address the ball – I'm using the driver here, but you can just as easily start by teeing-up with a mid-iron to give yourself some confidence. As you start your takeaway, say "one". When you get to the top of the backswing say "two". Then as you swing down, say "three" the moment you feel you are striking the ball. Let's go through this again together. "One" starts the backswing, "two" signals the change in direction from top of backswing to start of downswing and "three" is...bang!...impact.

Even if you don't actually say it to yourself as you hit shots, it's a great idea to say it in your mind as you take your practice swing before each shot. It's things like this which help you keep your rhythm going during a round – just when you don't want lots of swing thoughts cluttering your head. If you're not quite sure of this method, apply it to my swing; or someone else who swings it slow, such as Fred Couples, next time your watching a tournament on television. You'll see how it works with every club in the bag, and this should give you the confidence to try it yourself.

Address the ball and say "one" to start your swing...

..."two" signals the change of direction from the top...

...and "three" as you nail that ball into the distance.

Or the simple 1, 2

If you're a fast-talking, fast-walking type of person, then you'll probably prefer a brisker, more upbeat tempo to your golf swing. If that's the case then the 'numbers game' will work for you, too. But instead of counting to three you need to stop at two.

Let me explain what I mean. As you start your backswing, say "one". I then want you to feel that you say "two" at the exact moment you strike the ball. Okay, let's do it again now. "One" as you start your backswing and "two" as you hit the ball. As I mentioned in the previous drill, even if you don't go with this method for shots on the golf course, it is a particularly good drill to build into your practice swings.

If this "one-two" method does sound good to you, then there's no better role-model for you to watch than Nick Price. Next time he's on television, watch him hit shots – say to yourself, "one" as he starts his backswing and "two" as he rips through the ball. You'll start to appreciate how well it works – and how easily you can convert this formula into your own game. This will help keep the tempo of your swing exactly the same for every shot you hit. And that really is the key.

What I'm telling you here is only a guide. Don't take it as gospel and feel free to experiment with the rhythm of your swing. The most important thing, however, is that when you do find a swing speed that's comfortable, work like mad to maintain it. It makes your bad shots less bad and your good shots great. And that's a prize worth sweating for.

Once again, say "one" to trigger your takeaway...

...but for a quicker rhythm to your swing, say "two" as you rip the clubhead through the ball.

How to Hit Big

Seven secrets for more distance off the tee

Ever since I was about 15 or 16, I've been able to give the ball a pretty decent 'rip' off the tee, although when I play in a tournament I usually keep 20–30yds (18–28m), maybe more, in reserve. That surprises a lot of people. But how I see it is that I'm easily long enough off the tee for any golf course, and by swinging at, say, 80% of my full power, I feel it gives me just a little bit more accuracy and control. Put it this way, I'd rather be in the centre of the fairway than 30yds (28m) further, and in the rough. I think every golfer would.

Unfortunately, I don't see much evidence of this strategy in the pro-ams I play in. More often than not, my playing partners are practically jumping out of their golf shoes in an effort to launch the ball as far as is humanly possible into the distance. One-in-five drives might come off, resulting in a potential birdie. But the trouble is, the other four are usually unplayable and probably cost a double-bogey, or even worse. That is not the kind of ratio that will help you shoot a good score.

Let me reiterate what I said in the chapter on driving: hitting the ball a long way has nothing to do with muscle-power and brute force. Sure, I'm a big, tall guy and that certainly helps. But it's good, solid technique, not size and brute force, which sends the ball a long way. Look at Davis Love III, you certainly wouldn't describe him as a muscle-bound, power-house and yet he's one of the top-five longest hitters in the world. Like I say, good technique, not brute force.

What I'm going to do now, then, is show you some really useful exercises you can work on which will improve your technique and help you focus on the correct feelings and sensations that promote good, powerful driving. This is distance the easy way. I won't try to kid you, though – you're not suddenly going to start hitting the ball as far as me. But these exercises can help you hit the ball your absolute maximum distance – which I reckon is a lot further than you currently drive the ball off the tee. Not only will you start hitting it past your playing partners, but before you know it you'll be reaching those par-5s in two shots, no problem. Take it from me, that's a lot of fun.

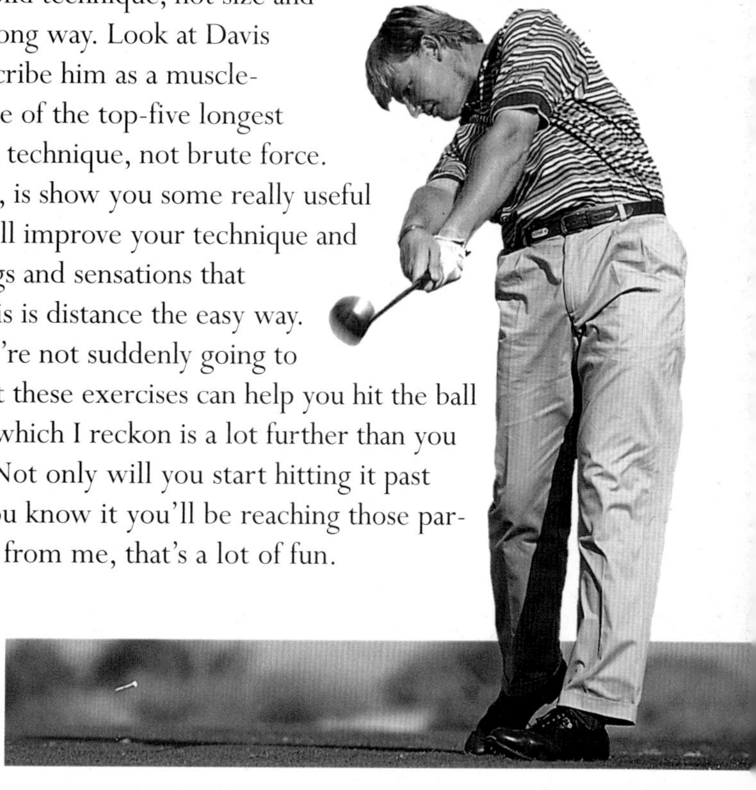

DRILL 1: Widen your stance and your takeaway

The first thing you have to say to yourself when you're shaping up to give the ball a mighty rip is "widen everything". That really is one of the keys to making a more powerful swing, generating more clubhead speed and seeing that ball launched further into the distance. So spread your feet further apart than you would normally, roughly 2in (5cm) further apart. That's going to give you a rock-solid base, which is just what you need to support what is, after all, the most powerful swing you can possibly make.

When your feet are incorrectly spaced apart, a whole host of problems will follow. If your stance is too narrow, for instance, there's no way you can generate power – you don't have any kind of base to support the turning motion of your upper body. You'll lose your balance, too, which is bound to do you a great deal of harm. If, on the other hand, your feet are too far apart the problems are equally serious. While you may not lose your balance, you certainly won't have any chance of making a complete turn. I don't care how supple you are, you're just not going to be able to turn your shoulders 90°. Again, that's going to hinder your efforts to create power.

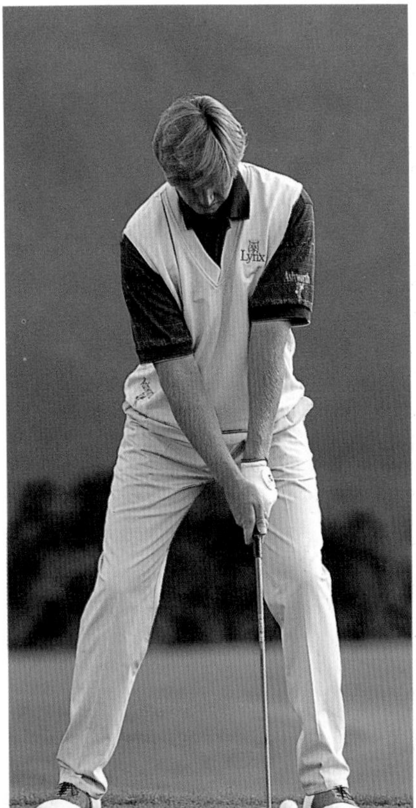

So once you're set up with that slightly wider stance, really sweep the club back as wide as you can. But don't go straight back – the club has to travel inside the line as it goes back. And be careful not to 'hood' the clubface, either. I see some amateurs do that when they're trying to make a wide backswing – they reach back, which is good, but the clubface looks at the ground for too long and that causes problems later in the swing. Just stretch it out as wide, and as slow, as you can get. The hands stay passive – all you should feel is your left forearm rotate, slowly but surely, keeping the clubface square to the path of your swing.

Once again, remember to keep your rhythm – just because you're going to hit the ball further, it doesn't mean to say you have to swing faster. In fact, in the early stages of the swing the complete opposite is true. Think low and slow and feel your left shoulder turning under your chin and your arms pulling your left side behind the ball. Now your swing is on the right track – there's width and rhythm. And this good start really is going to help you hit the ball a lot further.

DRILL 2: Turn your back on the target

Set up with nice posture.

Turn your back on the target.

And generate maximum power.

Distance comes from clubhead speed, but that's only half the story. It is far more accurate to say that distance comes from clubhead speed that is correctly applied. And you can only apply clubhead speed correctly if your technique is solid.

So don't fall into the trap of swinging faster when you want to hit the ball a long way. Because the chances are that if you swing faster then you'll probably swing more raggedly, too. You'll lose control and that costs you not only distance, but also accuracy. Short and crooked: I'm not sure that's a combination I like the sound of!

To summarise. To increase your clubhead speed and hit the ball further you have to swing the club better. And that means training your body to work correctly in the swing.

One of the keys I like to think of to help me make a better swing, and ensure that my upper body behaves correctly, is to turn my back on the target in the backswing. It's that simple, but it's a highly effective swing thought. It helps make sure that the big muscles in my body are fully wound up, ready to spring powerfully back towards the ball in the downswing.

Try it yourself. Set up to the ball with your driver, with nice posture, and then focus on turning your back on the target in the backswing. Now you're getting the big muscles in your body – which are hugely effective assets when it comes to creating clubhead speed – playing their part in the power-generation business. Remember, power doesn't come from the hands alone. Try throwing a golf ball without moving your body and you'll see what I mean.

I like the feeling this simple exercise gives me. Once I'm in this fully wound-up position behind the ball, I'm in great shape to really unleash the power in my swing into the back of the ball. There's lots of clubhead speed and, just as importantly, it's correctly applied. That makes for a combination of long and straight, which I like far better than short and crooked.

DRILL 3: Hover the clubhead for mega-speed

Bernhard Langer does it with his irons. Greg Norman does it with his driver. So does Sam Torrance. I'm referring, of course, to the business of hovering the clubhead above the ground at address. Let me explain to you what I feel are the benefits of this method. Because even if you decide not to introduce it into your game permanently, I really believe it's well worth making it a regular part of your practice routine.

Again, I'm using the driver because here we're dealing specifically with hitting the ball further. But as I said, Bernhard Langer hovers the clubhead with his irons as well. To be honest, if it feels right, you can do it with any club.

It's a very simple process. Just address the ball with your driver and hover the clubhead above the ground. Not by much, just enough so that it sits squarely behind the ball. This will improve your swing for several reasons. For one, it will encourage a smooth first move away from the ball. Can you see what I mean – I know it's tough to appreciate in still photographs, but the club is moving away from the ball on a wide arc, nice and smoothly. Low and slow, as I often like to say. This gives me the crucial width that I need in my backswing, which means the clubhead is going to travel further in the swing, on a wider arc. And that means the ball is more likely to travel further as well.

Try it and you'll feel exactly what I mean. Because there is no interference from the turf, you're more likely to keep your takeaway smooth – there's nothing to interrupt the flow of the clubhead away from the ball. This can only be good for the rhythm of your entire swing.

Going back to the example set by Bernhard Langer, I would say that if you can get used to it, then the case for hovering your irons is even greater than with the driver. You see, the trouble with grounding your irons behind the ball is that it is easy for the clubhead to nestle down a touch. And from anything longer than a closely-mown fairway, the clubhead can easily get 'snagged' in the grass, causing you to snatch the first part of your takeaway. That's going to upset the rhythm and co-ordination of your swing.

So, even if you don't feel that this is something you can introduce into your game 'full-time' it's still a great practice drill to get you used to the feeling of making a smooth first move.

Hover the clubhead...

...sweep it away low to the ground...

...to encourage better impact.

DRILL 4: Wait for it, then let it rip

Let's talk a little bit about the downswing again. One of the mistakes I see a lot of amateurs make when they're looking for extra distance is snatching the club from the top (sorry to dwell on my poor pro-am partners' mistakes, but they're fairly representative of the problems most club golfers have). The weight moves across to the left side too abruptly, which destroys the co-ordination between the arms and body and this all contributes to making the downswing too narrow and too cramped. Golfers who are prone to this fault probably hit a lot of low, squirty, cut-shots out of the heel of their driver. Okay, so it's not the most destructive shot in golf, but it's not exactly pleasing, either.

If this sounds horribly familiar (and you find you're wearing a hole in the heel of your driver!) then it's time to go to work on driving a better, more powerful downswing. One that lets you hit the ball more solidly and produces those all-important extra yards off the tee.

Just for the purposes of this exercise, I'm going to split the downswing into two stages. As you may have guessed from the title of this exercise, the whole idea is that you 'wait for it' (that's the first stage) then 'let it rip' (that's the second).

Swing into a fully-wound position at the top.

Settle your weight in the downswing.

Let's first get you into good position at the top again. Really stretch your upper body round in the backswing. Turn your right hip behind you and feel the muscles in your lower left back pulling tight as you swing the club to the top. Get your left shoulder under your chin. Remember, it's just like coiling a spring. The more you twist it, the faster it unwinds...and the more power you can create.

Now start your downswing by shifting your weight back towards your left foot. Don't slide your legs, though. Start to transfer your weight and feel as though you unwind your upper body. And don't hit, or snatch, from the top. That's where you get too steep, which kills distance as sure as anything. Just 'settle' yourself and feel like you leave the club behind you – just 'wait for it'.

Once you're in this kind of position, in good balance, you can really 'let it rip'. Start to pour on the power and hit the ball as hard as you like with the right hand. Sense that your head 'hangs back' behind the point of impact, all the way through impact. Just as you can see me doing here. The club is moving so fast through the 'hitting zone' that it pulls my arms and body through into the followthrough position. If you can keep your balance throughout, then you've cracked it. You'll hit the ball real solid and it will fly higher and carry further.

This, you will not be at all surprised to hear, feels great!

Then you can pour on the power.

DRILL 5: Become master of the weighting game

'Weight transfer' is an expression you hear frequently when golfers or teachers talk about the golf swing. Like a lot of 'golfspeak' though, it can be a little vague without a full explanation and demonstration of the methods behind the words. In any sport – it doesn't matter whether it's tennis, boxing, baseball, even throwing a ball – you have to transfer your weight in order to generate power. It's not enough to simply stand there and swing your arm. The body has to play its part. To demonstrate: first, the simplest movement of all – throwing a ball. Look what happens when I do this. I start with my feet firmly planted and as I draw my arm back, my weight transfers back over on to my right side in harmony with the movement of my arm.

Then as I bring my arm forward to release the ball, my weight simultaneously shifts over on to my front foot. If I didn't do that, the ball wouldn't go far. Yet this happens naturally without me even having to think about it.

The same is true in boxing, another of the more instinctive sports. Look what happens when I throw a punch. Again, my weight moves back as I load up – then forward as I deliver what could be the knockout blow. There's power there only because I've got my weight behind the punch.

If you're copying me now, you'll realise that in all of these actions, you don't really have to think about the role of your body. It behaves quite instinctively as your arm moves back and forth. The golf swing isn't such an instinctive, natural movement, but the theories are exactly the same. You can't generate power unless your weight is in harmony with the swinging movement of your arms and the club. That's what is meant by good weight transfer.

At the top of the backswing, my body has turned and my weight is over my right foot. I am loading-up the spring so that I can unwind with maximum speed. At this point you should almost feel that you could lift your left foot off the ground and not fall over.

As I swing my arms and the clubhead towards the target, my weight has also moved towards the target. That's how you pack a punch off the tee. It is a gradual process, which comes to an end with virtually all of your weight supported over your left foot.

HOW THIS ACTUALLY AFFECTS YOUR *GOLF SWING*

The key to good weight transfer is to flow with the natural progression of your swing. Where the clubhead goes, your weight goes with it. In the backswing your weight must move back on to your right side in harmony with the swinging motion of your arms. At the top, the majority of your weight should be over your right knee, loaded-up like a boxer ready to deliver a punch or a cricketer ready to hurl a ball in from the boundary fence. Gradually, but purposefully, your weight should then move over to your left side in the downswing and through impact.

A common fault that can destroy your entire golf game is the reverse pivot. This happens when the weight moves towards the left as the club travels back. Then, in the downswing, the weight lurches back on to the right side – in totally the opposite direction to the swinging clubhead. From this position, you have no chance of success, except maybe of redesigning the fairway with a rather natty, criss-cross pattern, or hitting those guys over on another hole.

Once again, for as long as you play this game you must remember that if you fail to transfer your weight correctly, you have no hope of making a good coil – and without that there will be no power at all.

DRILL 6: Learn to sweep low and slow

Lack of loft on a club tends to intimidate lots of golfers. I know, because I can see the evidence in their swings. The most common sign of this is the golfer who tries to help the ball into the air. This stems from a lack of confidence in the club's ability to generate the necessary height – they sit the club in behind the ball, see hardly anything of the clubface, and hit the panic button. They stay back on the right foot and, failing to transfer the weight in harmony with the swinging arms, try to scoop the ball into the air. The result is usually the complete opposite of what the golfer intends to do – a topped shot along the ground or else they catch the ground long before the clubhead reaches the ball. Either one is pretty disastrous.

There are also plenty of golfers who suffer from the other extreme. They don't see much loft on the clubface, either, but they favour the brute force-and-muscle approach. Clenching their teeth and strangling the grip, they're trying so hard to smash the ball as far as possible and into the air that they come down on it too steep. They're outside the line, chopping down, and from that position they can really hit just about any shot in the book – except a good one, that is. With good technique you don't have to help, or smash, the ball into the air. The loft on the club will do that for you. Your only part of the deal is to swing it. With the long clubs, then, the message is you've got to learn to sweep the ball away. In that crucial 24in (60cm) or so just before and after impact – the hitting zone – the clubhead should be travelling real low to the ground. This ensures that you hit the back of the ball with the correct amount of loft.

Sweep the club away smoothly... *...and then back and forth through the hitting zone.*

To help you appreciate this sensation – because it is bound to feel strange at first if you've been swinging a different way for years on end – try the exercise that I'm demonstrating here. Grab your driver and stand to the ball. Now make mini-swings back and through, just above the ball, as one continuous movement. Get the feeling of the clubhead sweeping back away from the ball – low and slow – then sweep it through the impact area – again, low and slow.

Now from this point just in front of the ball, recoil and sweep the club all the way back to the top of the backswing. This is one of the keys to this exercise, so repeat it again. Move the club back and through, mini-swings remember, to a point roughly 2ft (60cm) ahead of the ball. And from there, sweep the club all the way back to the top of the backswing. Rehearse this as many times as you like. Then, when you're ready, start the movement all over again. Only this time, don't stop at the top of your backswing. Continue all the way into your downswing and nail that ball into the distance.

This exercise will definitely help you create a wider arc in your swing, and I reckon you'll make a better coil in the backswing as well. You'll also get used to the feeling of the clubhead sweeping back away from the ball and sweeping through the hitting area – shallowing out your angle of attack.

These factors are all going to combine to help you hit those long clubs more solidly and, if you can master these, you'll never again have any problems getting the ball airborne off the tee – take my word for it.

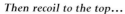

Then recoil to the top... *...and swing down smoothly, sweeping the ball away, finishing in perfect balance.*

DRILL 7: Keep your chin up

Don't be mislead here, I'm not talking about keeping your chin up in the psychological sense – such as straight after a double-bogey on the 1st hole, for example. No, I'm talking about curing one of the most misleading bits of advice in golf – the phrase "keep your head down". It really does make me want to cringe when I hear someone say this to their playing partner and I reckon it does ten-times more harm than good. In my experience, when someone is told to keep their head down, they tend to bury their chin into their chest at address. From there, they can't possibly make a good turn in the backswing as there's no room for the left shoulder to turn into. And no turn means no power.

Together, right now, we're going to blow that piece of advice right out of the water, once and for all. So I want you to banish forever any thoughts of trying to keep your head down – it really is nonsense. Instead, I want you to think more in terms of keeping your chin up. Look at me here and I'll demonstrate to you what I mean.

Still using your driver, address the ball as you would normally. Now, keeping everything else as it is, lift your chin up 2in (5cm) or so further away from your chest –

You can see here in the photograph above the problems of trying too hard to keep your head down. It all looks far too cramped. Far better to keep your chin up at address, as I am doing on the left. You almost need to feel as though you're looking down your nose at the ball.

far enough so that you feel you're almost looking down your nose at the ball. I know this may well feel strange at first, but stick with it my friends because the advantages in the swing are well worth it.

Firstly, and most importantly, it gives your left shoulder all the room it needs to turn under your chin – essential if you are to coil your upper body correctly in the backswing. This has the knock-on effect of helping you transfer your weight correctly in the swing, too. Put together, this makes it easier for you to achieve the things you need to achieve in order to create power in your golf swing. As I stated right at the start of this book, golf is a chain reaction – if you make a better backswing you immediately boost your chances of making a better downswing. And then you're really in business.

By keeping your chin up away from your chest, you create plenty of room to turn your left shoulder in the backswing, as you can see from the photographs of me directly above and to the right. The inset at the very top shows that when my chin is too close to my chest, I struggle to make anything like a full shoulder turn. So will you.

Shaping the Ball

How to hit draws and fades

The first thing I want to stress to you in this chapter is that if you can grasp the fundamentals of the golf swing, then shaping the ball at will through the air should not be a problem. That statement is probably going to surprise a lot of you, because the fact is, most amateur golfers that I come into contact with don't even think about shaping their shots. I think there are two reasons why this is the case.

First, and most commonly, the average player thinks it is too advanced for him. Well that's wrong for a start. Sure, shaping the ball at will is nigh-on impossible if you don't know what you're doing. But if you know how, and why, the ball swerves through the air, controlling that movement is not half as complicated as you might think. You are certainly capable of making it happen.

Secondly, a lot of golfers think that there's no point shaping the ball unless there is something blocking the way, like a tree. I've got news for you. In a single round of golf, Jack Nicklaus will often shape every single iron shot he hits, depending on the pin placement. If the hole is cut on the right side of the green, he aims at the centre and fades it in towards the flag. If the flag is on the left side he again aims at the centre, but this time draws the ball in towards the target. If the ball flies straight, he's dead centre. And with everything going according to plan, Jack's looking at another birdie. That's smart golf – increasing the margin for error. So no, shaping the ball isn't just for getting around obstacles. It can help you hit more greens and fairways.

There are basically two types of shaped shot: the draw, which moves the ball right-to-left; and the fade, which moves it from left-to-right. Let me show you how to hit both of these shots, and also give you some advice about using them at the right time to help lower your scores.

The draw – a class shot for all seasons

The situation that I've found myself in here is tailor-made for the draw shot. I've got 180yds (163m) to the green and the tree is too tall for me to fly over it. I've got to go around it, in this case, following a right-to-left route. There really isn't much of a problem for me – and soon it won't be for you, either!

The first thing you have to do is close your stance. That means your feet, hips and shoulders all need to be aligned right of the flag. But not the clubface – that needs to be aiming pretty much at the target. Also position the ball a fraction further back in your stance than if you were hitting a regular iron shot.

From here you can go ahead and feel that you make a normal backswing. You don't need to make any changes – your address position has taken care of that for you. Setting-

Align your feet, hips and shoulders right of target. The clubface is closed.

up in this way means the clubhead is travelling well inside the line on the way back, which is exactly what you need when you're looking to move the ball right-to-left. This results in a top-of-the-backswing position where the club is pointing right of the target – as you can see is the case from the photograph overleaf.

From the top, you really need to feel that you attack the ball from the inside. Sense that your right elbow drops down to your side as you start your downswing – that puts you on the right track. Plant a picture in your mind of the clubhead travelling from in-to-out through the hitting zone – in other words, along the line of your feet. Use this mental image to encourage the correct swing path, because that's what slings the ball out to the right.

Through impact, feel that your right hand crosses over your left. Really release the club freely – you might try gripping a little more lightly than usual, as some players do, to encourage this free-flowing movement. If it helps, try to make the toe of the clubhead

Take the clubhead back along the line of your body.

pass the heel as you strike the ball. All of these images help you generate the correct clubface positioning, closed in relation to the path of your swing, and this is what creates the draw-spin that brings the ball back to the target. One other thing that you need to bear in mind is that the ball runs a little more on landing than it would with a regular iron shot, so make sure you take this into your calculations.

Well, that's pretty much all there is to playing the draw shot. Obviously you have to practise these techniques to enable you to control the exact amount of ball-swerve, but hopefully I've helped you realise that shaping the ball in this way isn't just the preserve of professional players.

And let me emphasize again that you don't need to be behind a tree to shape the ball. I want you to get into the habit of trying to shape your shots into greens – perhaps not in the next monthly medal, but certainly in your next practice round. Hold the ball into the wind, seek out tight pin positions behind bunkers – above all, make the ball work for you. If you can develop this talent, it's going to add a few extra strings to your bow and make you a far more accomplished golfer.

The clubshaft points right of target at the top.

The clubhead travels on an in-to-out path through impact.

Release the club freely through the ball.

And finish in a nice, rounded position.

MEMORABLE SHOTS – THE 1994 WORLD MATCHPLAY FINAL, WENTWORTH

All of the factors I've just explained to you on drawing the ball, I used to stunning effect against Colin Montgomerie in the final of the 1994 World Matchplay Championship. I was two-up on Monty playing the 16th, but I'd pulled my drive a touch. Anyone familiar with Wentworth knows that left is bad news on the 16th, because the corner of the dogleg blocks your path to the green. To make matters worse, I was in the rough which makes it harder to shape a shot because grass gets between the clubface and the ball. Losing that hole would have thrown the match wide open, so I needed to make something happen.

Using the techniques I have just explained, I played it just as I had planned. The ball started fully 30yds (28m) right of the green and then began to move right-to-left through the air. It pitched short of the green, ran up the slope, and up onto the putting surface to 8ft (2.5m). That slammed the door shut on Monty's challenge. It left him having to make birdie to keep the match alive – he failed and the title was mine.

The fade – a left-to-right 'soft' option

The fade is a shot favoured by a lot of professional golfers. It's easier to hit than a draw, possibly a little more consistent and, the main reason for its popularity, it makes the ball sit down nice and softly. Essentially, it's a 'manageable' shot and I don't just mean for the pros. It's an easy shot for you to cultivate, too, and here's how to do it.

Not surprisingly, for a shot that goes left-to-right as opposed to right-to-left, the things you do to hit a fade are a mirror image of the techniques I just demonstrated for the draw. Your stance needs to be open – in other words, your feet, hips and shoulders need to point left of the flag. Once again, though, the clubface must still be square to your target and the ball needs to be a little further forward in your stance. Looking at me play the shot, over the next few pages, you can see clearly how open my stance is – and this puts me in great shape to 'shoot fade'. Again, once your set-up is correct you can focus your efforts on making a pretty standard backswing.

Your alignment automatically promotes an outside-the-line takeaway and this enables you to swing the club into perfect position at the top, where the shaft, hopefully, points left of target. In the downswing I want you to imagine the club swinging down on exactly the same path it travelled up on. Do everything I've told you to do in the downswing – unwind your upper body, smoothly transfer your weight on to your left side and maintain your original height – only this time, swing the clubhead across the line from out-to-in. Imagine that for those crucial 20in (50cm) before and after impact the clubhead is travelling on a line parallel with your toes. This swing path, combined with the open clubface, produces a shot that starts to the left of the tree up ahead, before fading back towards the target – a shot that you can really control.

Aim everything, except the clubface, left of target...

...and take the club back outside the line.

...so that the clubshaft points left of target at the top.

The clubhead travels out-to-in through impact...

...making the ball start left...

...before it fades back towards the target.

KEY TIP MAKE FULL USE OF THE TEEING AREA

Never just stroll on to a tee and simply place your ball anywhere. Put a bit of thought and imagination into it. By using different sides of the teeing ground you can make your drives a lot easier and eliminate the fear of trees, bunkers and water on some danger holes. You may well be surprised by how many more fairways you'll start to hit. Here's what I think is the kind of strategy you should look to adopt on the teeing ground, taking into account that it all depends on what shape shot you want to hit.

By teeing-up on the right-hand side of the teeing area...

...I can aim down the left and 'shoot fade', letting the ball work its way onto the middle of the fairway.

I like to fade the ball, so for me the right side of the tee gives me more fairway to shoot at. I can just aim down the left, shoot fade and let the ball work its way back into the middle. Ian Woosnam hits it the other way, so the left side of the teeing ground is going to give him more fairway to work his draw into. Whatever your natural shape, you can use the full width of the teeing area to make the fairway seem wider than it actually is. And personally, I don't think opportunities like that should be wasted, do you?

And by teeing up on the far left of the teeing ground...

...this allows me to aim down the right and play a draw, maximizing my target area.

"I hope I've succeeded in teaching you not just about the golf swing, but also about how to manage your game a little better and how to make sure that all your good shots count and your bad shots aren't too bad. So what are you waiting for? Get out there and practise..."

ERNIE ELS